UNIMPRESSED

MIRANDA TACCHIA

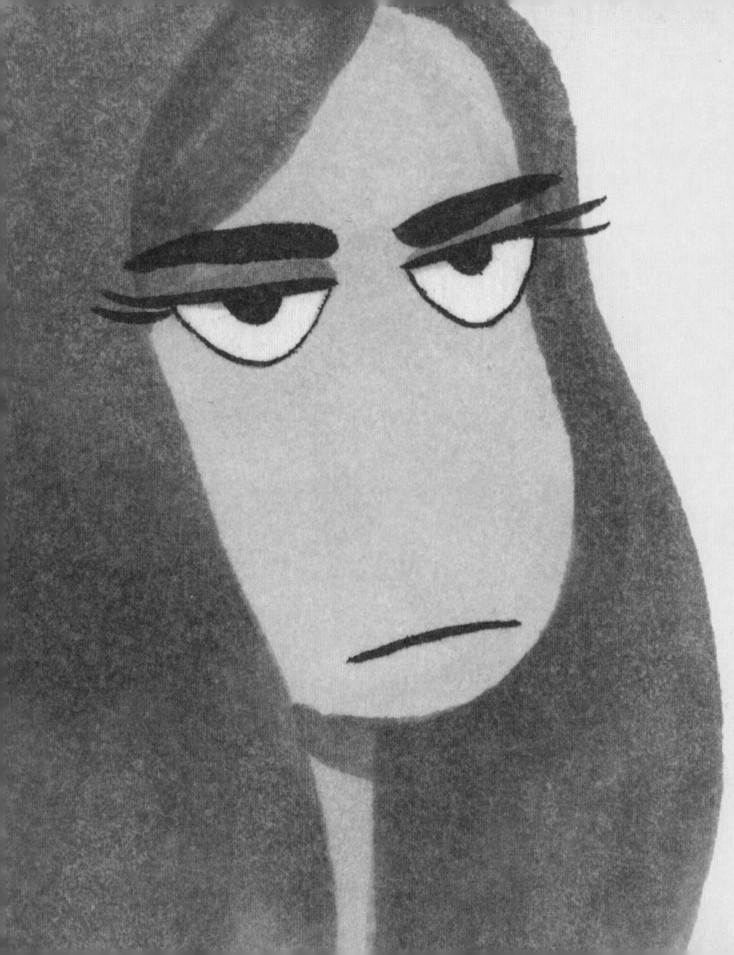

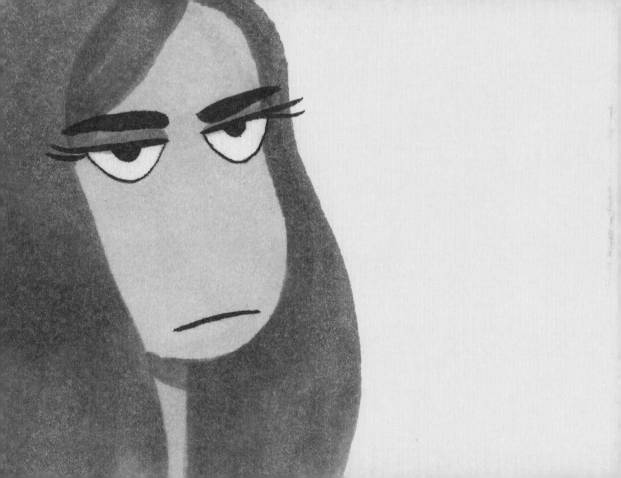

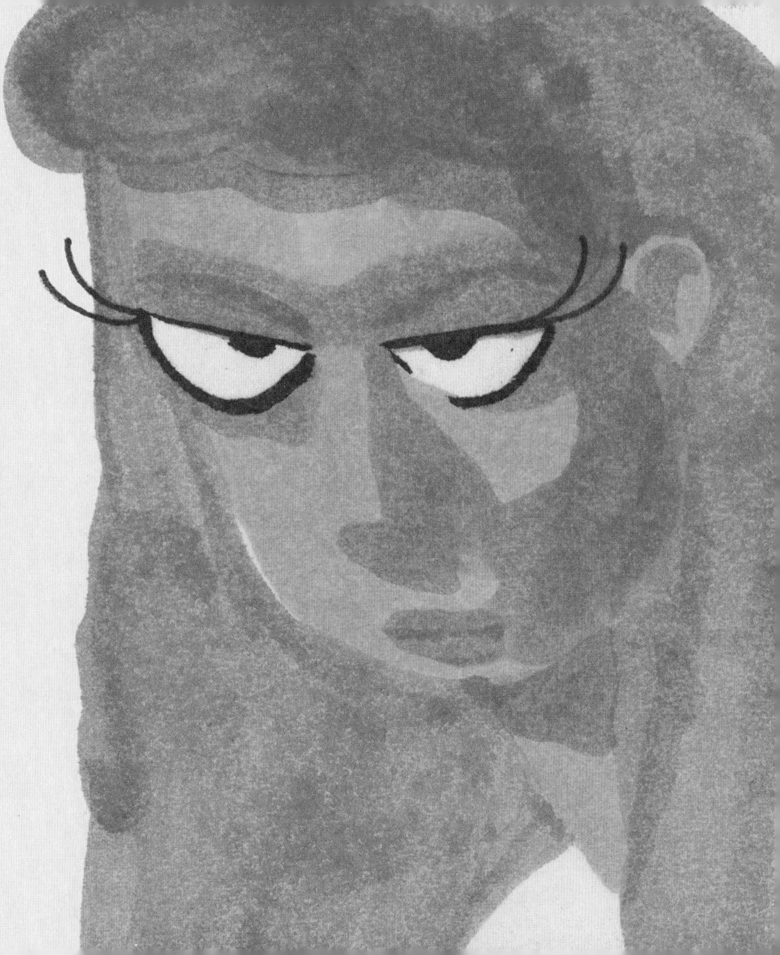

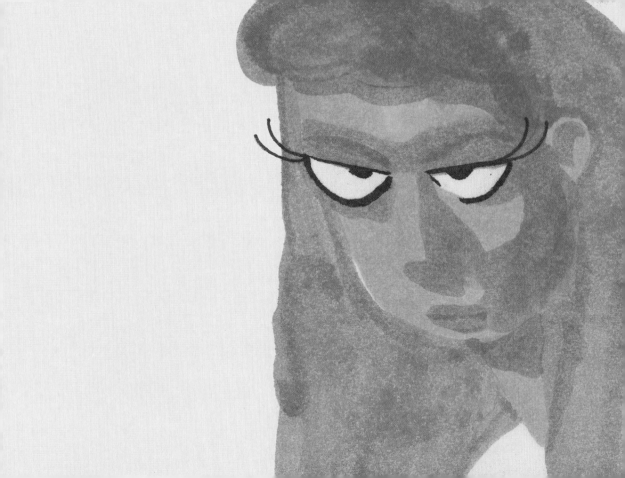

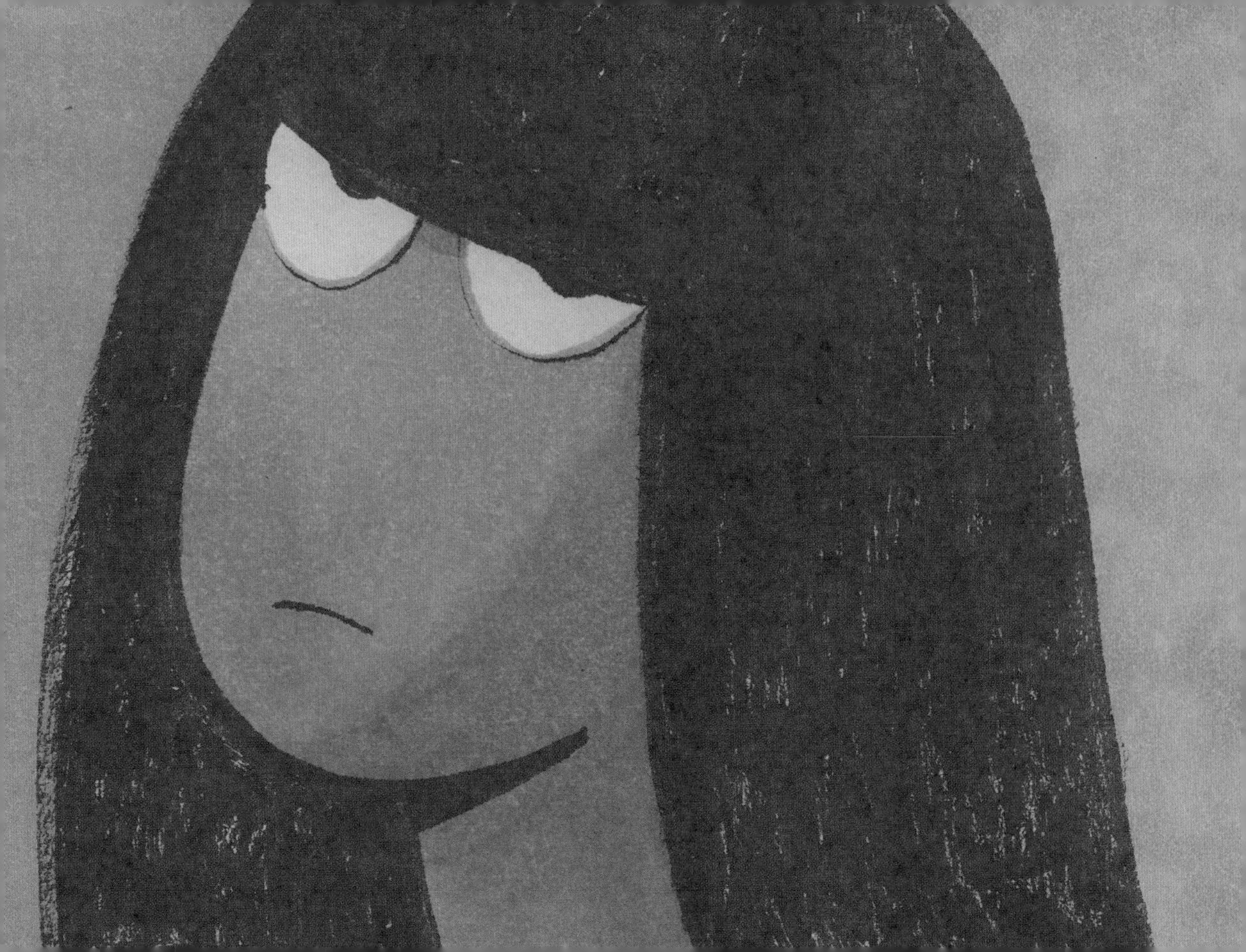

UNIMPRESSED

Miranda Tacchia

FANTAGRAPHICS BOOKS SEATTLE, WASHINGTON

CHAPTER 1

FRIENDSHIP

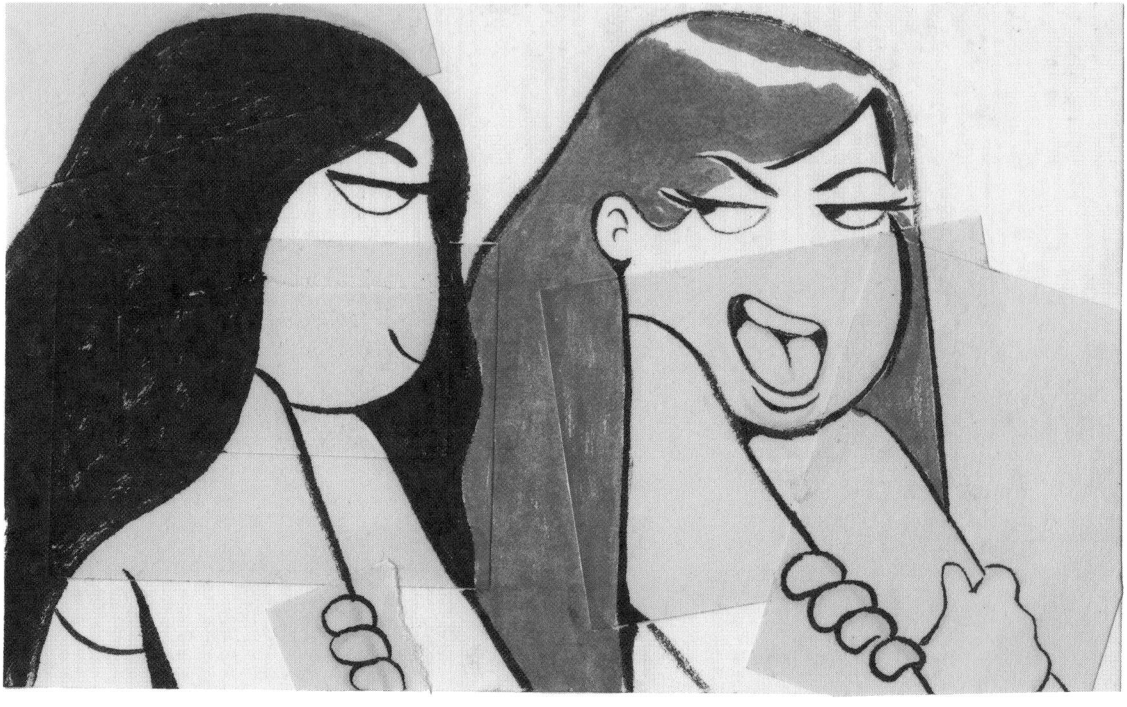

When you're both up to no good.

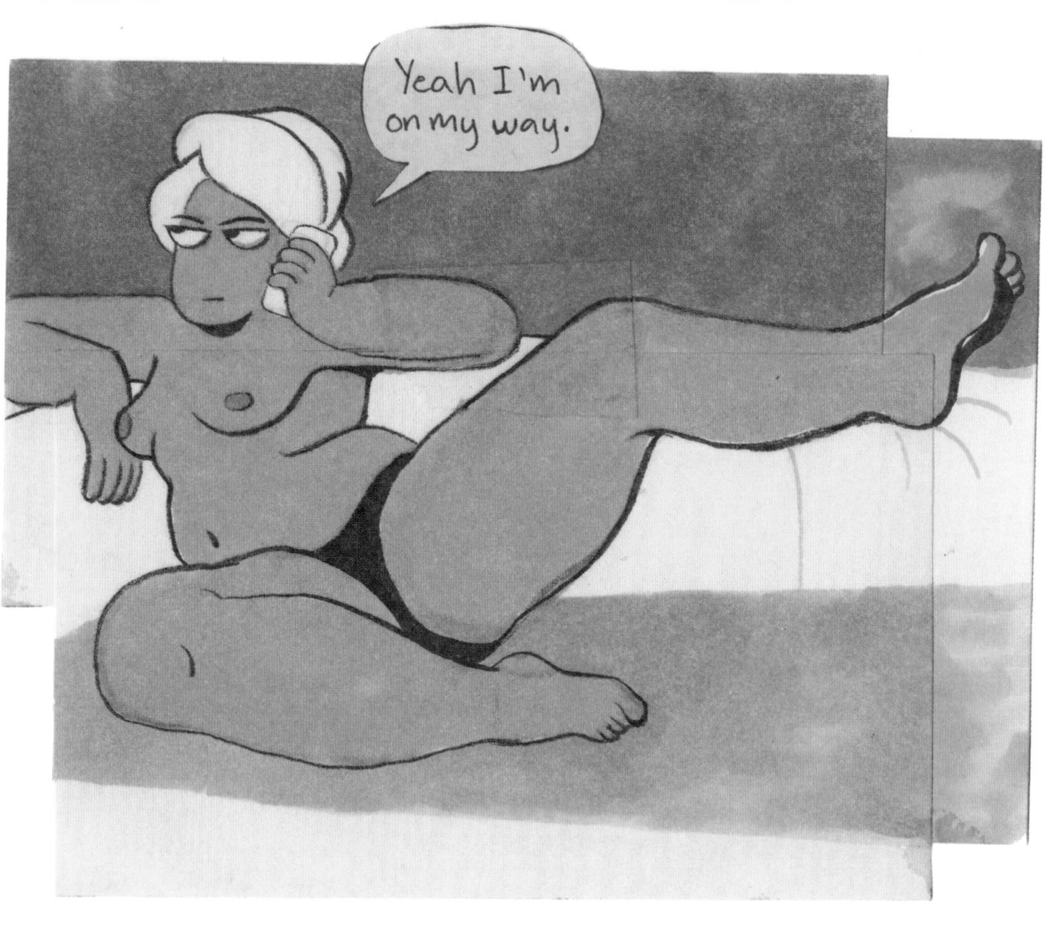
Yeah I'm on my way.

When you're just gonna be like,
5-90 minutes late.

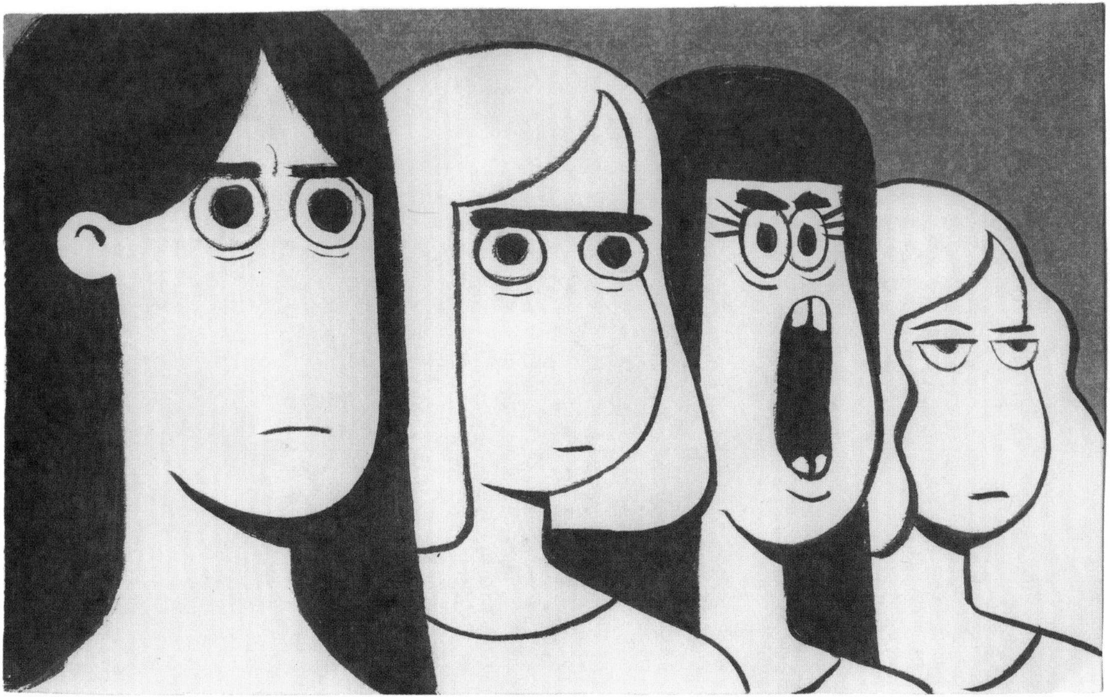

When there's one person in your group who likes drama more than everyone else.

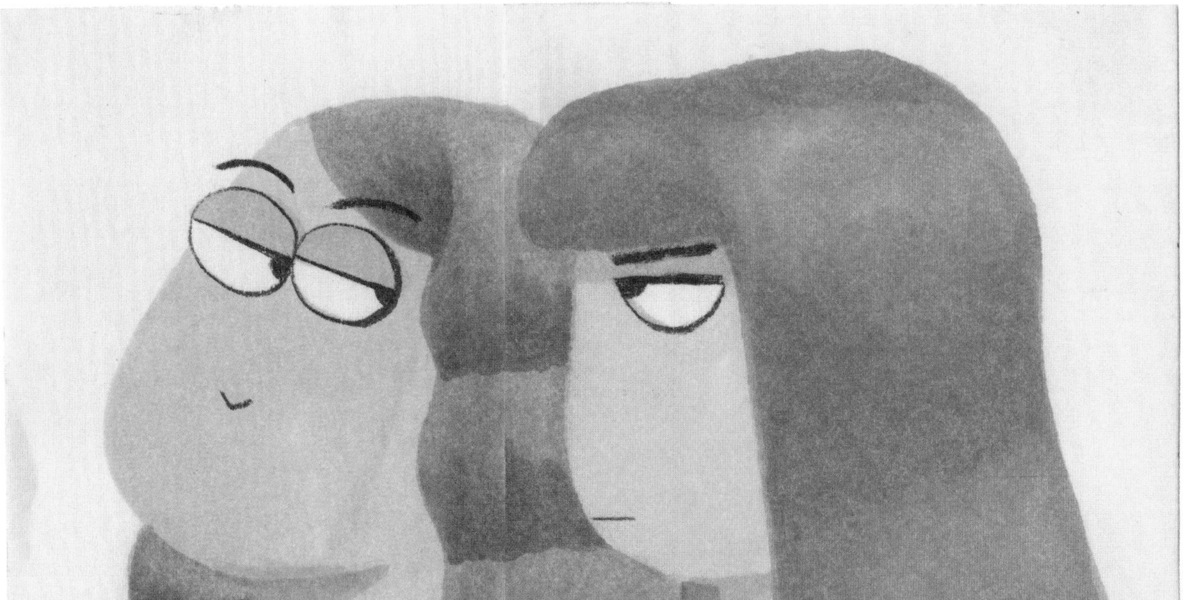

When you make a pun that tests the strength of your bond with each other.

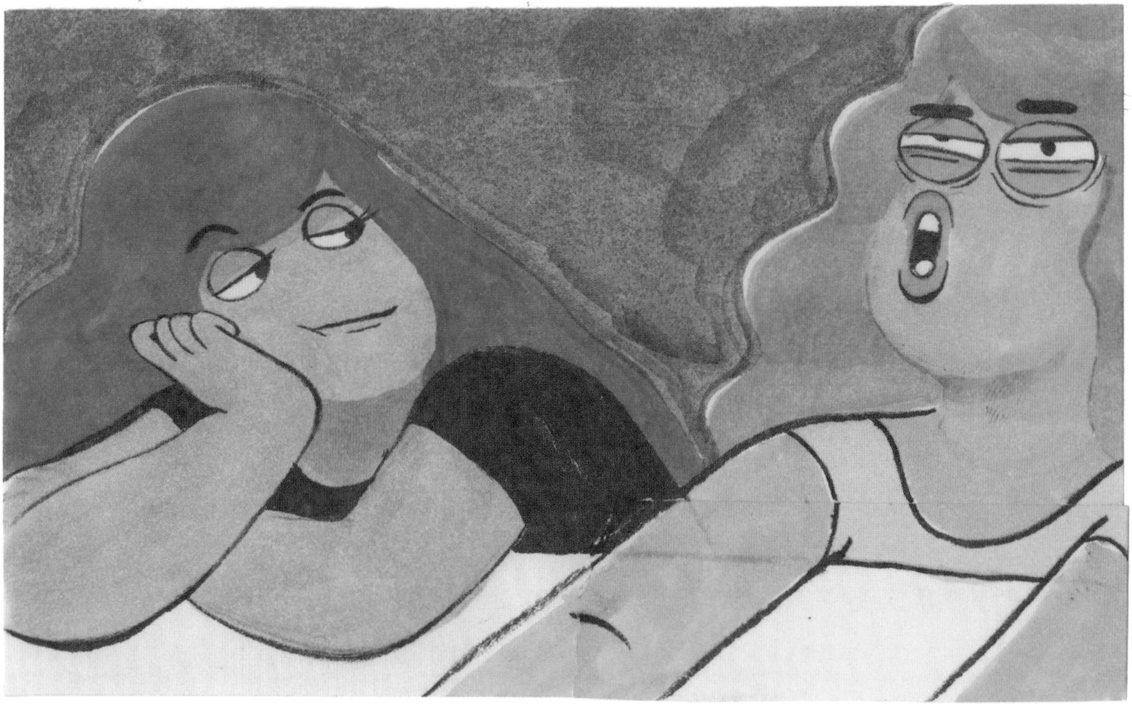

When you're both drunk as fuck.

When you just closed the door and your friend farts before starting the car.

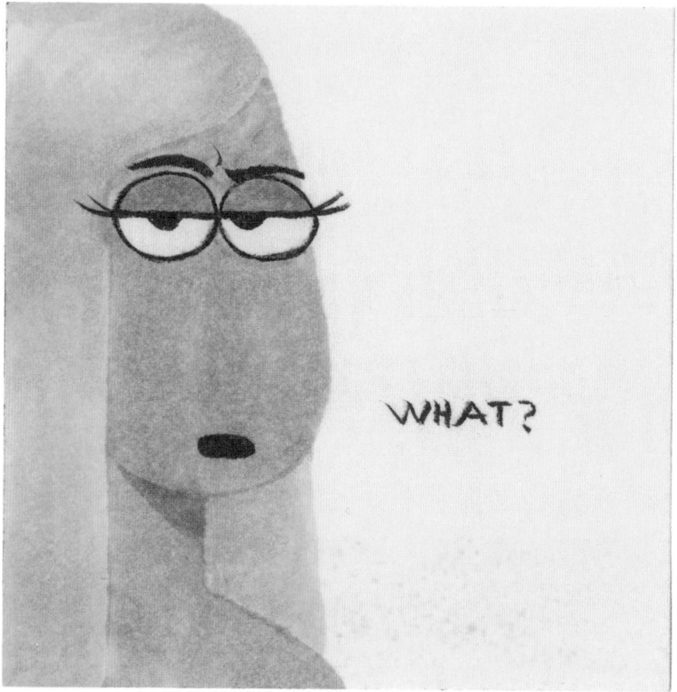
WHAT?

When you fart in your own car and your friend looks at you like it's some sort of fucking shock.

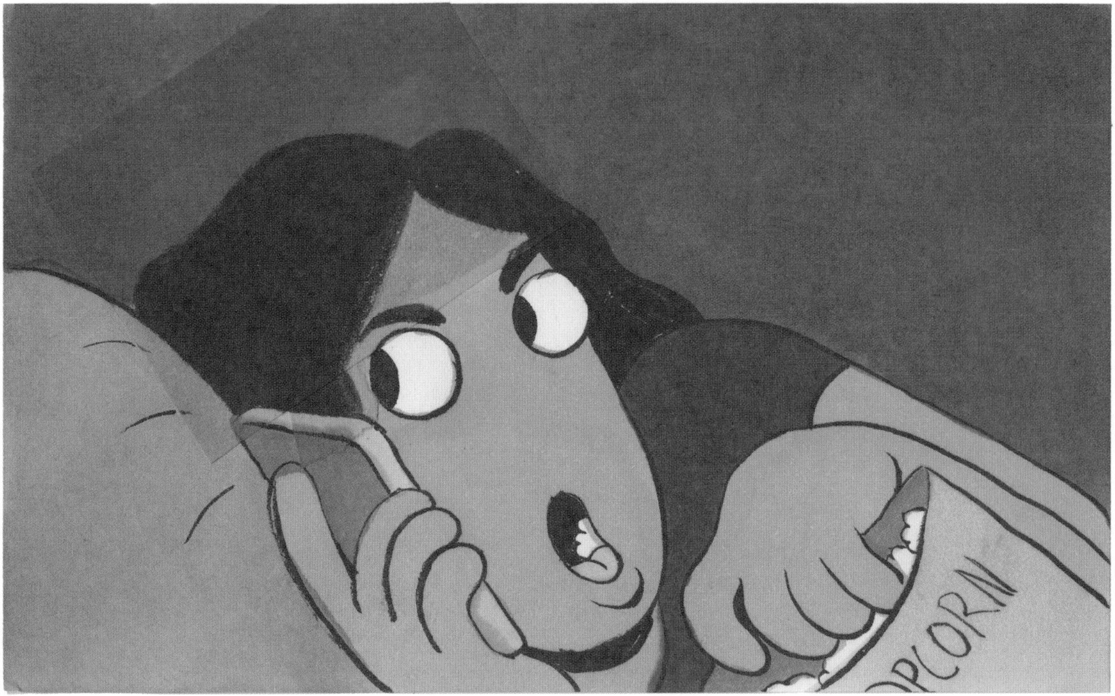
OPCORN

When you're listening to your friend
bitch about her problems and something
really dramatic happens on your favorite show.

When your friend invites you to a party you have no interest in attending and then asks if you'll drive.

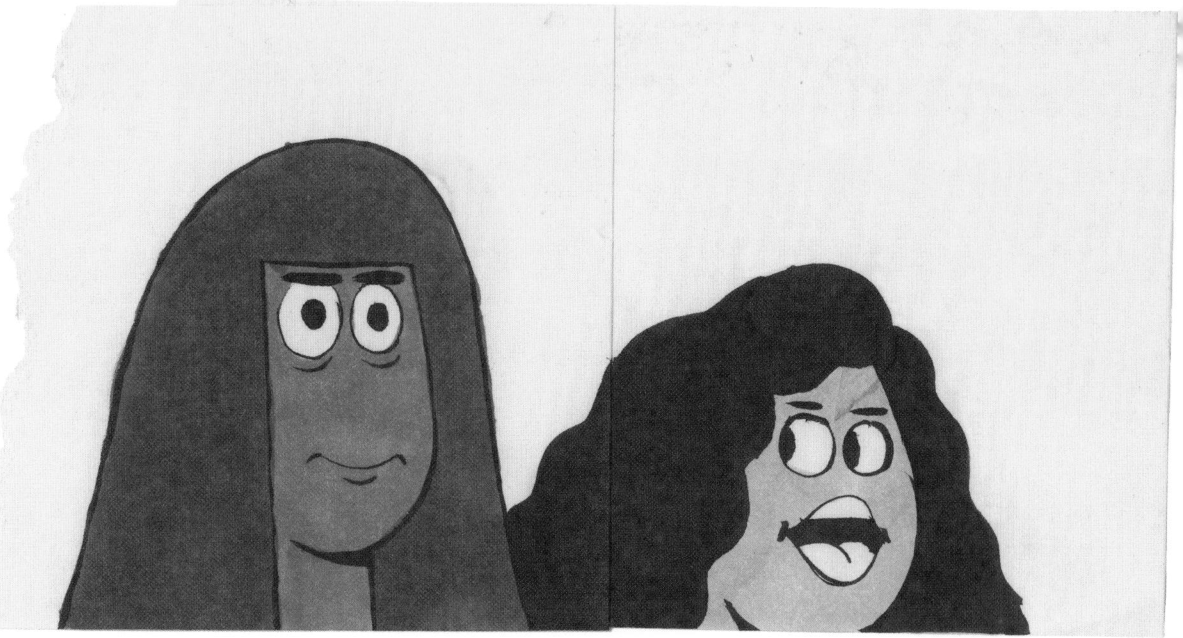

When you made a bet with your friend that you wouldn't argue with any dudes at the bar and your ex shows up.

When your friend takes a candid pic of you that you were like, not at ALL prepared for, whatsoever, in any way.

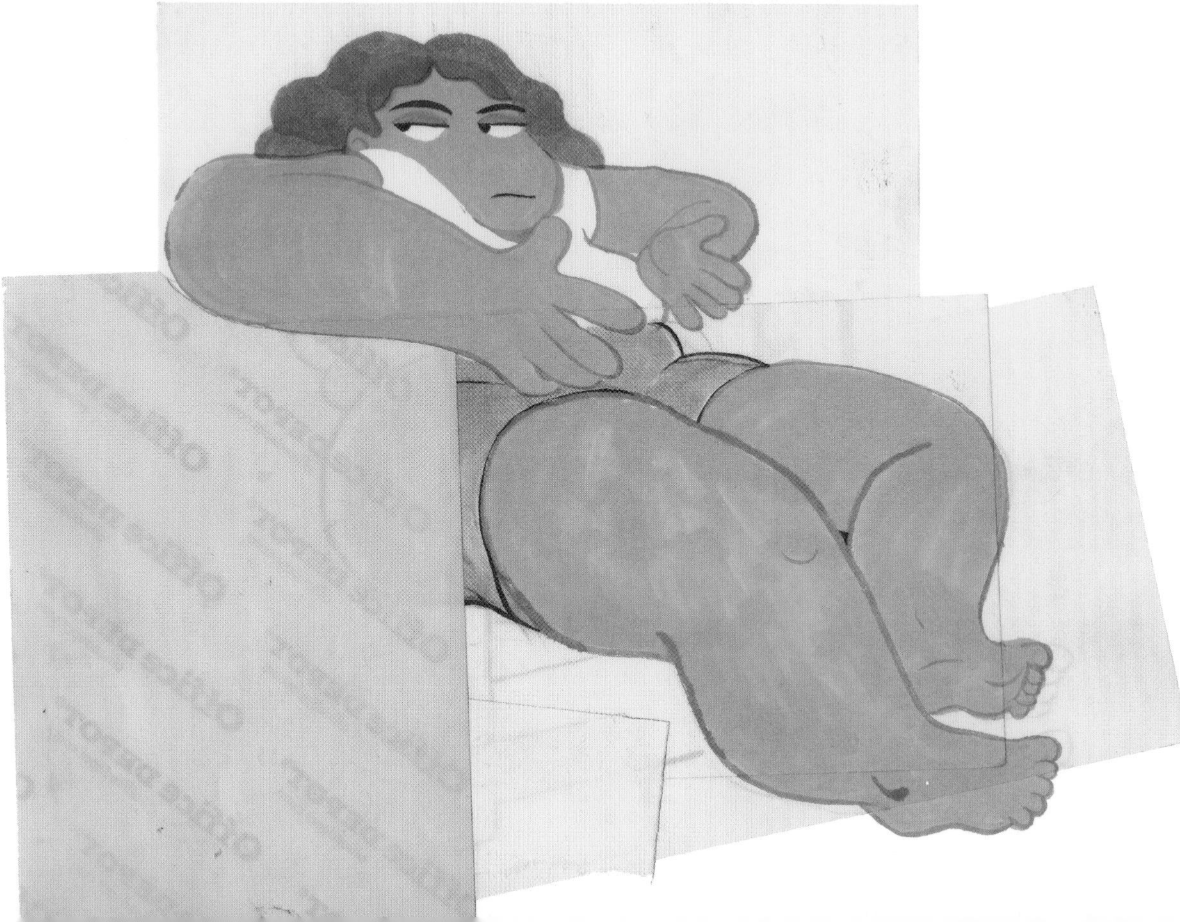

When your friend suggests something you said two minutes ago.

When your friend is jealous of your unrelenting
dad jokes and shitty wordplay.

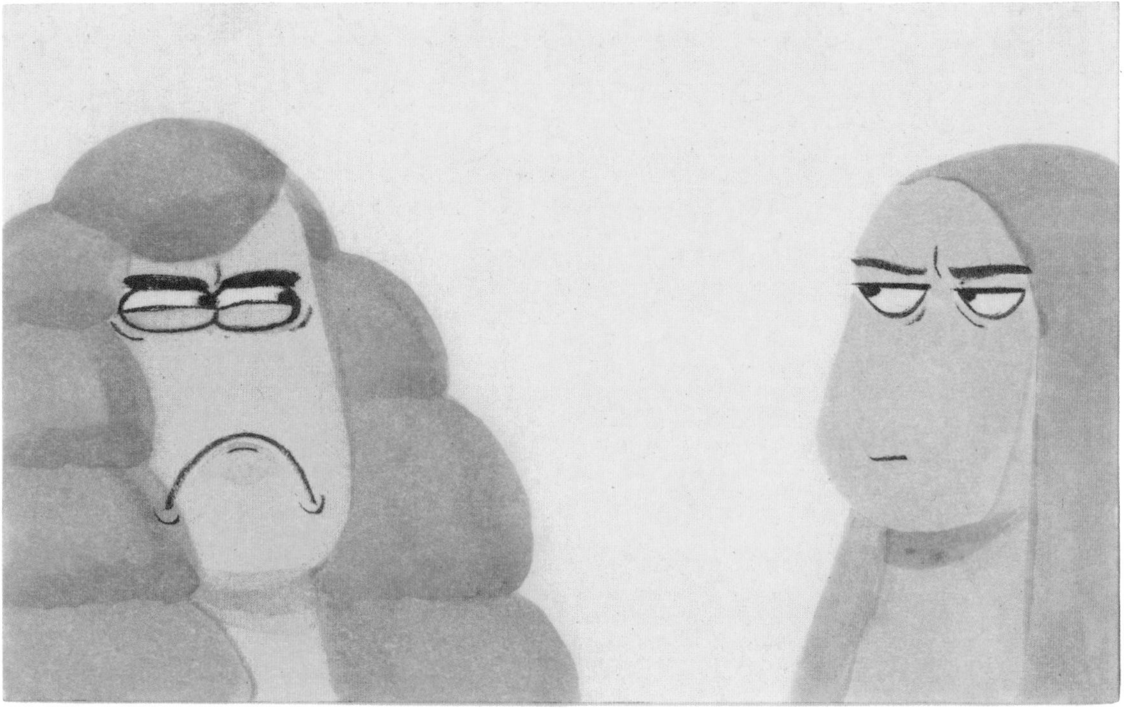

When you thought you were a bitch but you meet another person who's also a bitch.

When your friend convinces you to go out and then says she's tired.

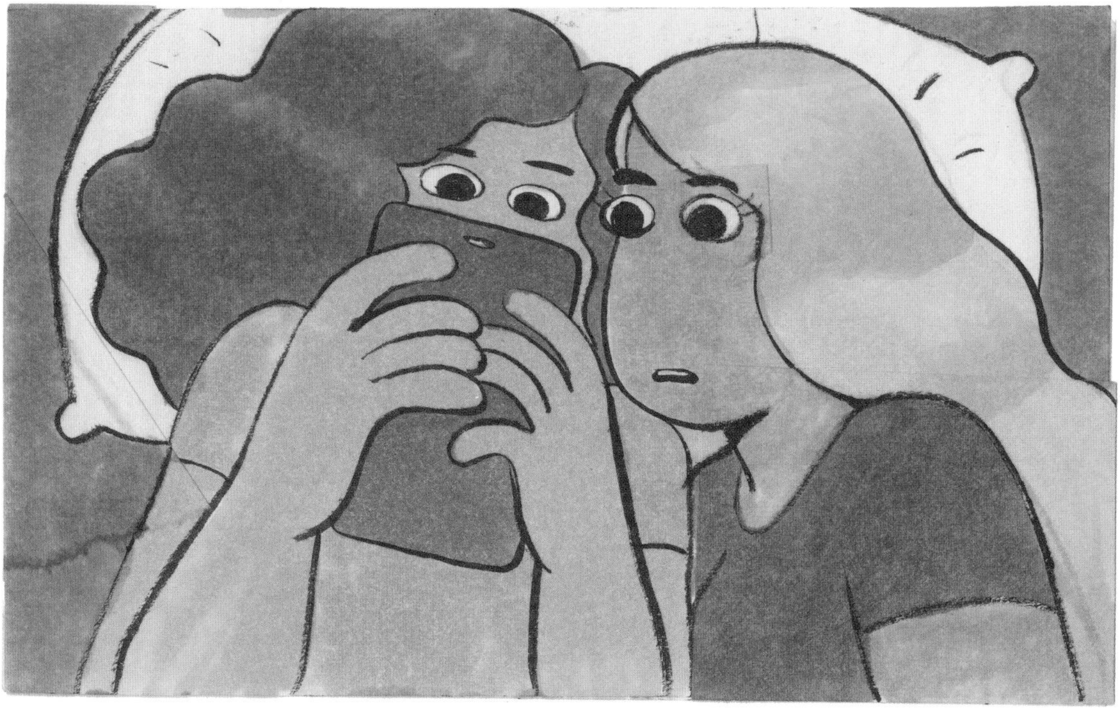

When you get a surprise dick pic
and view it with your BFF.

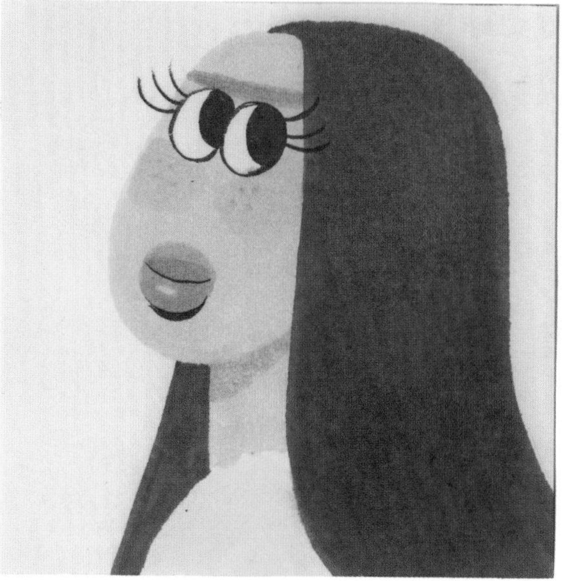
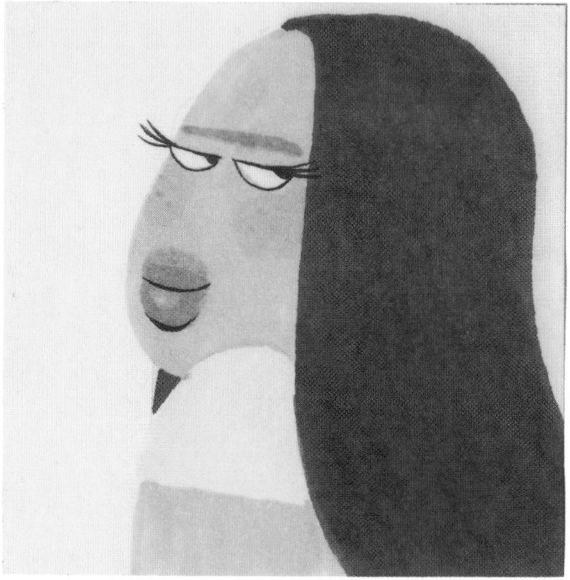

When your friend gives you a compliment.

When friends are everything.

When you get whistled at so your friend throws him off his bike.

When your friend is a lightweight.

When your friend is always right, even when she's not.

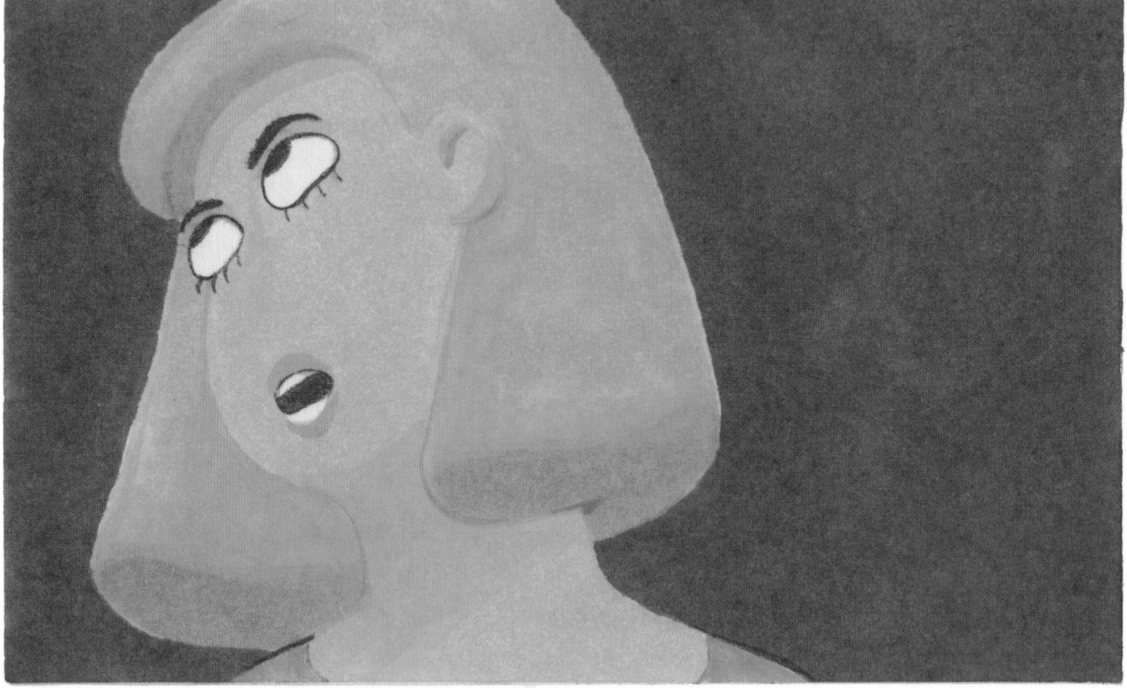

When your friend says she's ready to go
but you come back from the bathroom and
there's another margarita in front of her.

When you discover a piece of information that will allow you to scheme more efficiently.

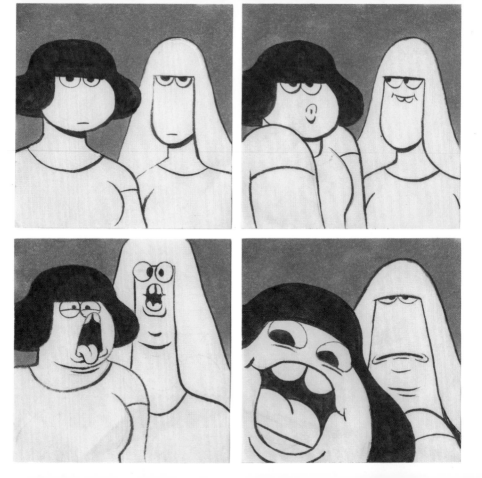

When you get in the photo booth with your friend.

CHAPTER 2
ROMANCE

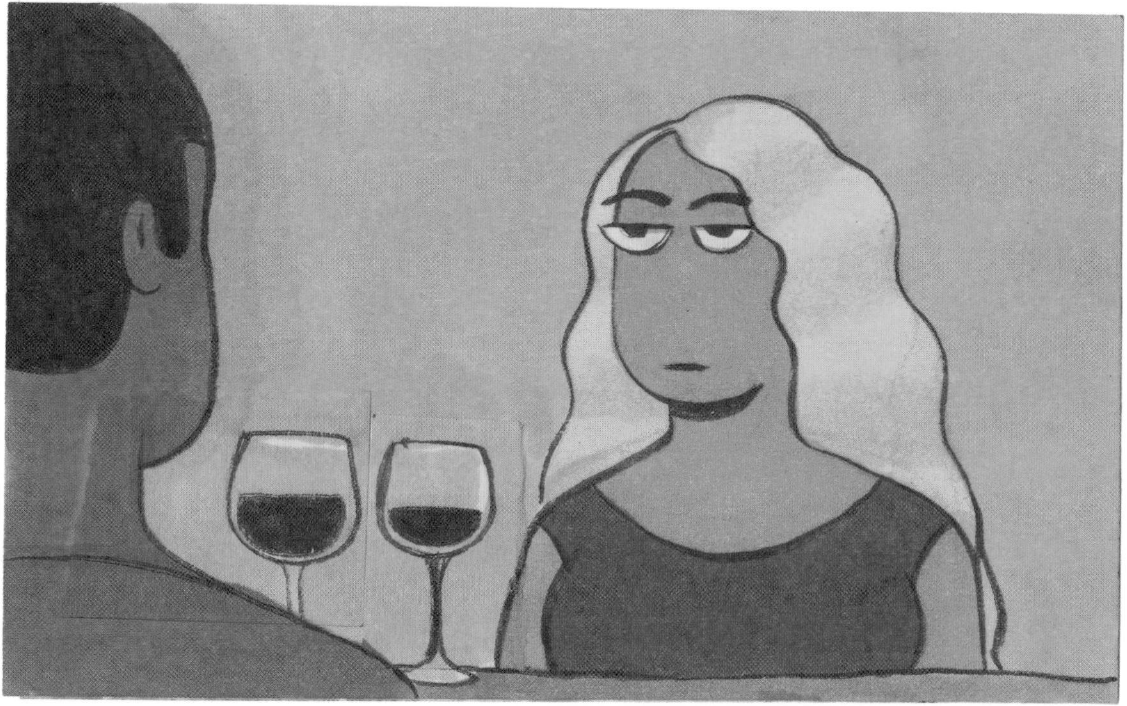

When you're on a first date and you hear
a blip on your bullshit radar.

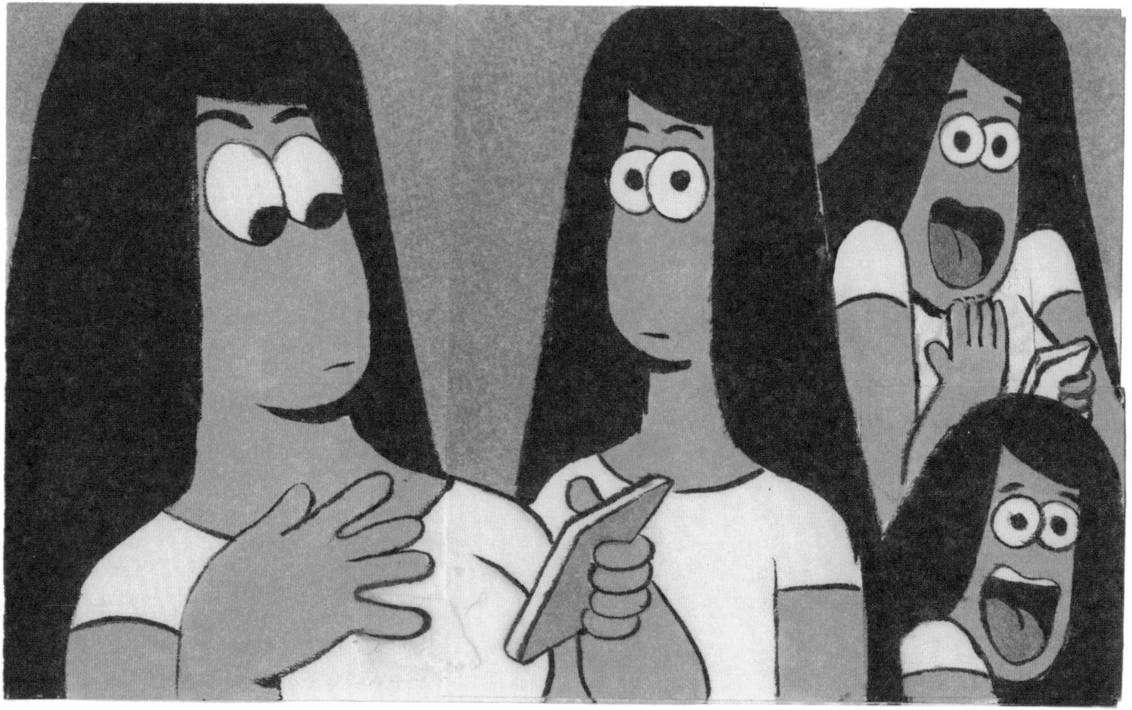

When he sends you that first dick pic.

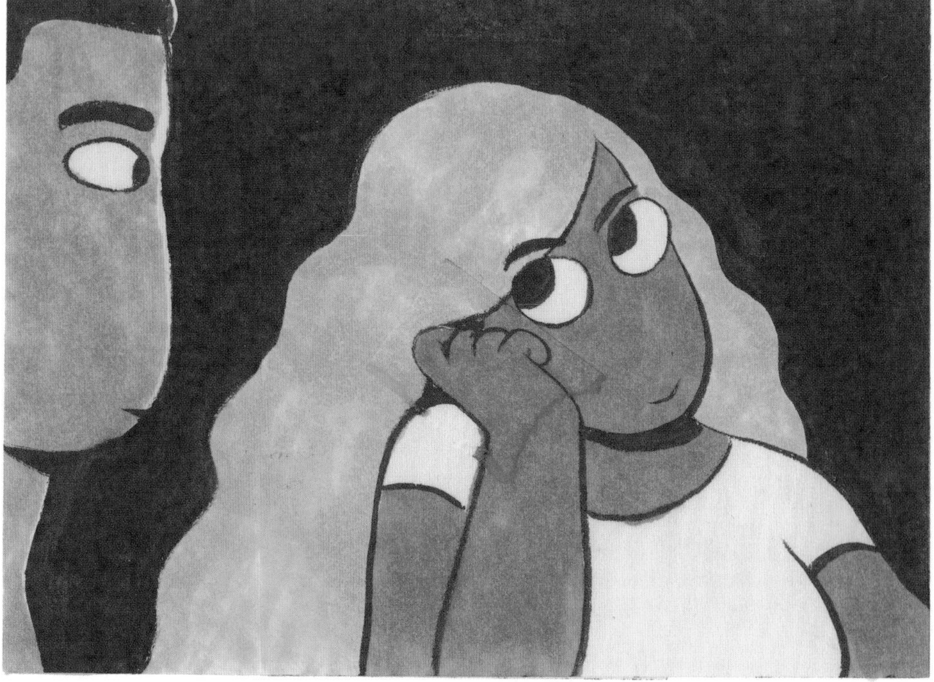

When you finally go out with your crush and then he asks what you're doing later.

When you're at his house for the first time
and the toilet won't flush.

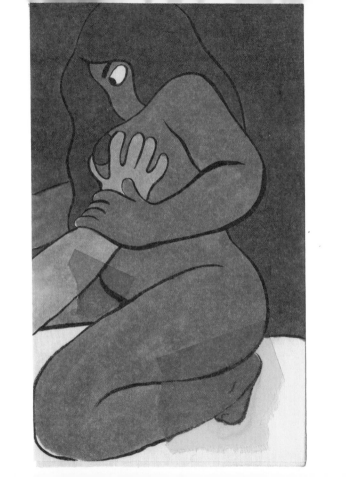

When he asks which movie you wanted to watch.

When he can't find the condoms.

When you've been on top for exactly three humps and he's already done.

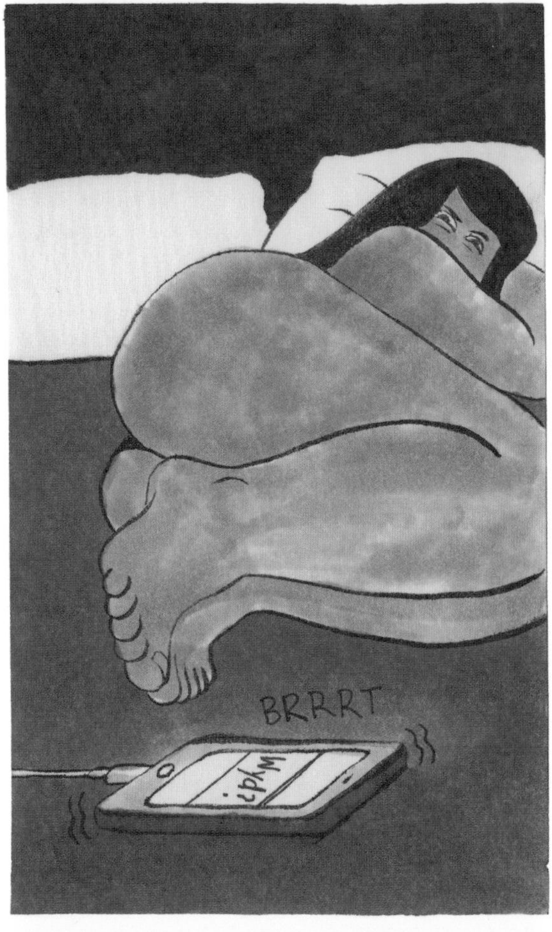
BRRRT
wyd?

When your dick appointment finally texts back after you fall asleep.

When you wanted it more than he did.

When he likes three of your selfies in a row.

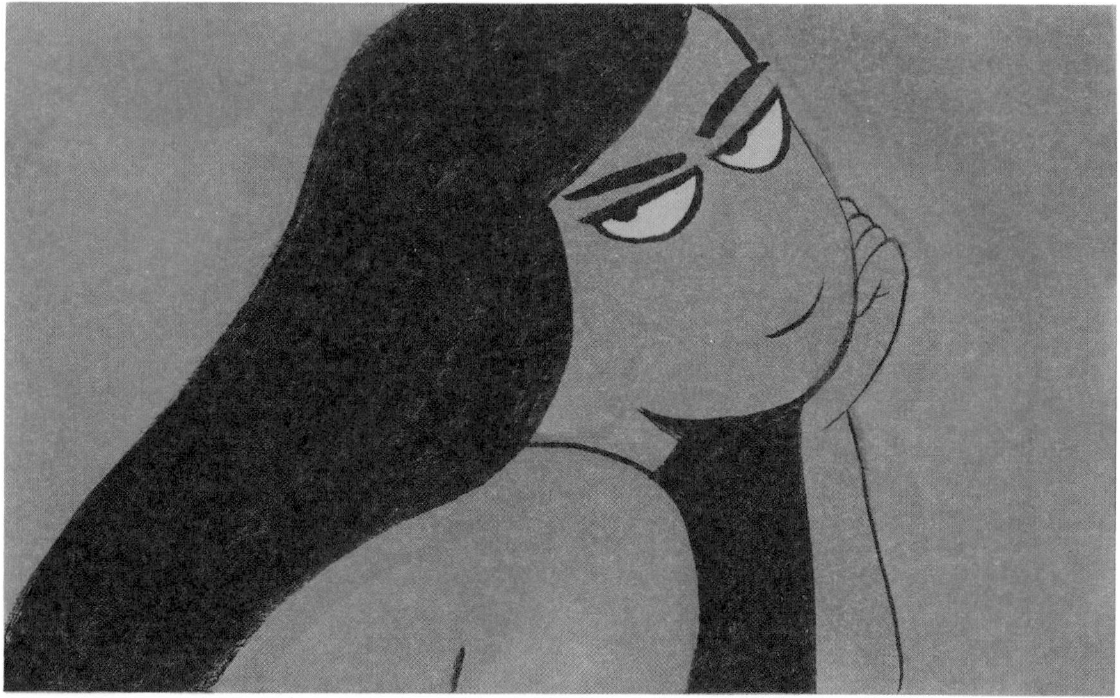

When he's smiling at your book collection.

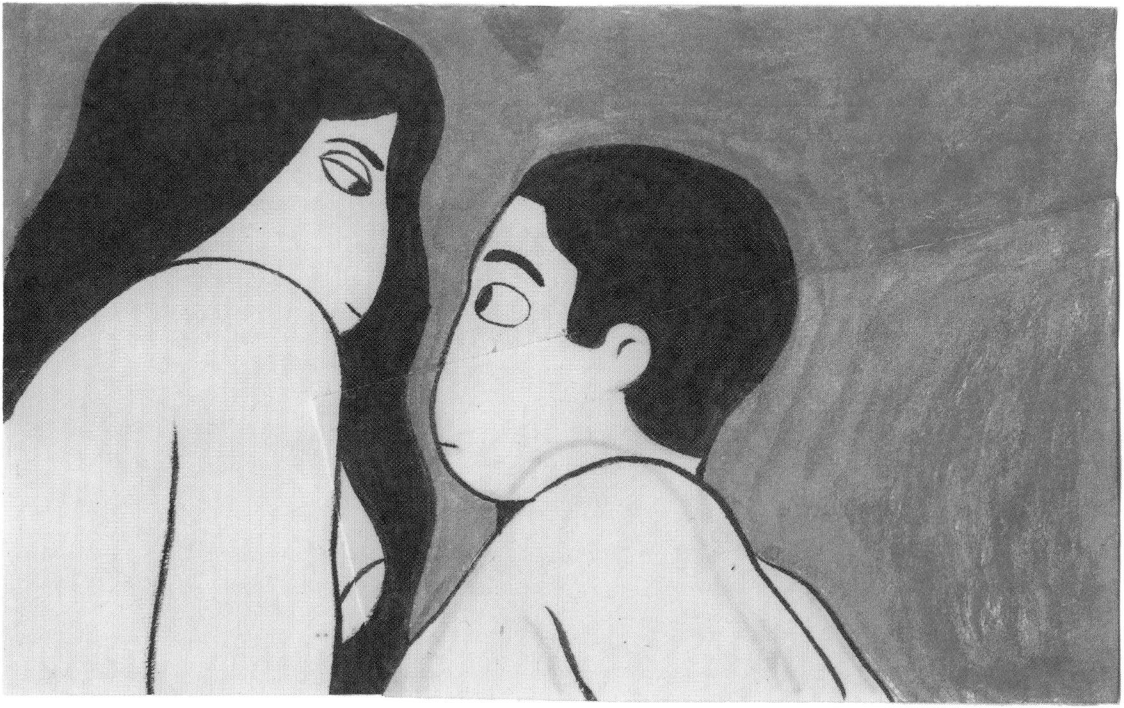

When you invite him over for a nooner.

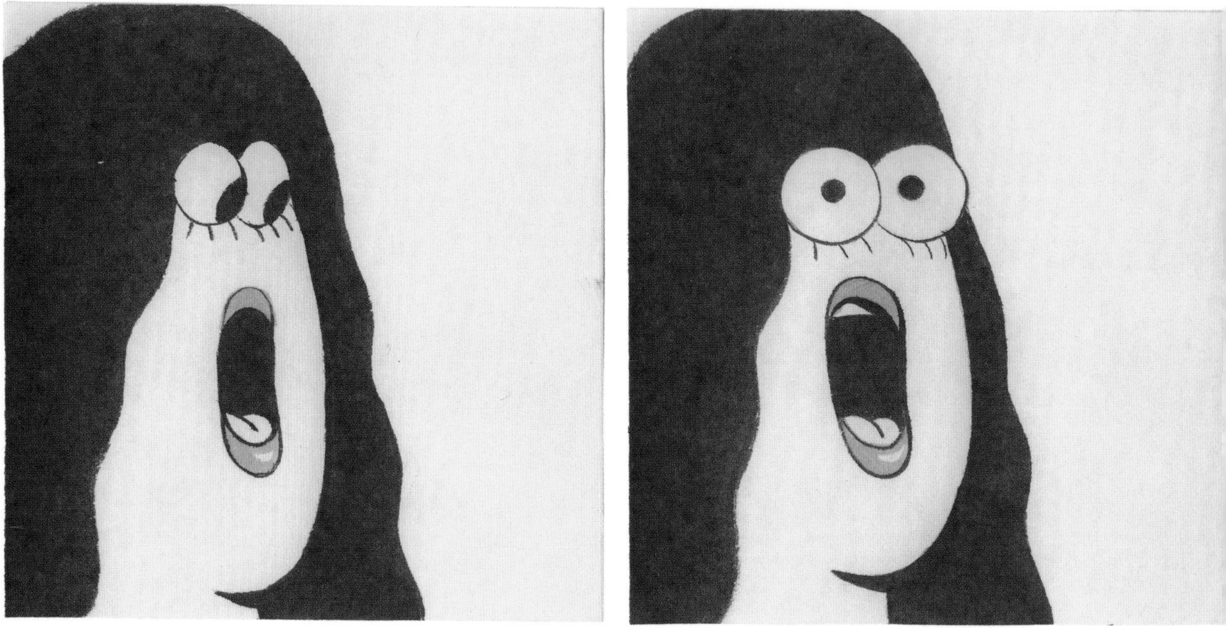

When it's way bigger than you anticipated.

When he tells you he doesn't eat pussy.

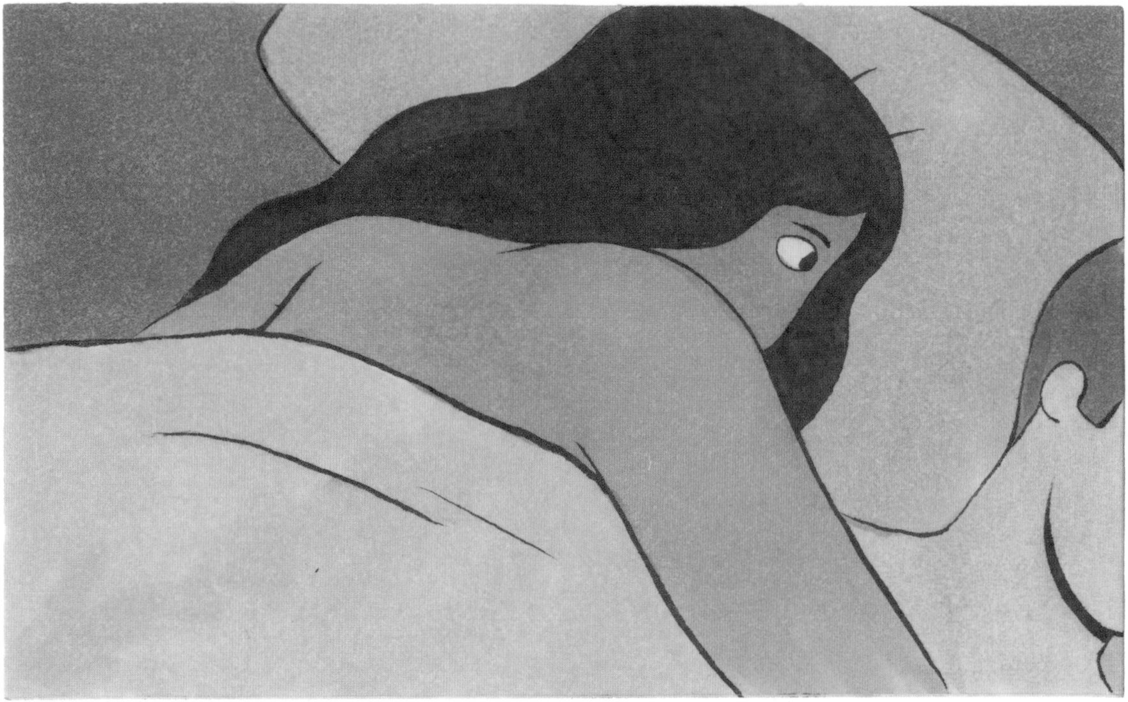

When it's a one-way street.

When you say no to a second date and he says "your loss" as he peels out of the parking lot, nut sack swinging to and fro on the back of his truck, like a douchebag pendulum.

When you get asked out on a date.

When you get him drunk without alcohol.

CHAPTER 3

DWELLING ON THINGS

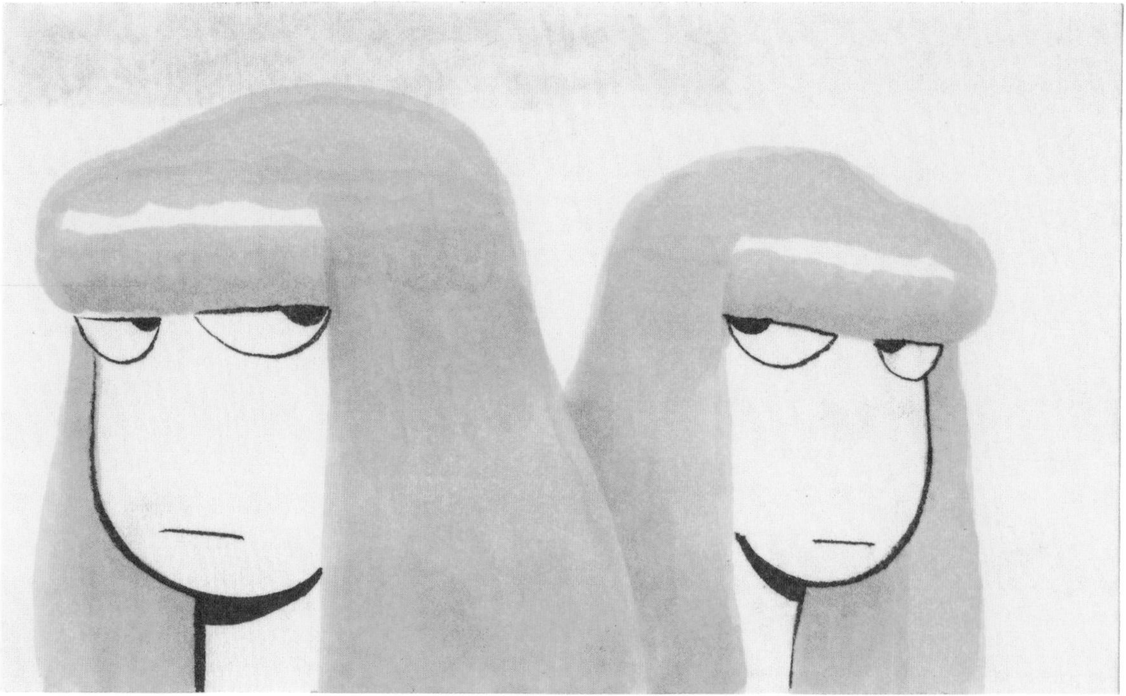

When you decide not to mingle because you're PMSing but you're kind of a cunt to begin with so it doesn't matter.

When you know someone's bullshitting.

When you're always at war with yourself.

When someone you don't like
is making a valid argument.

When you re-read that text from a year ago.

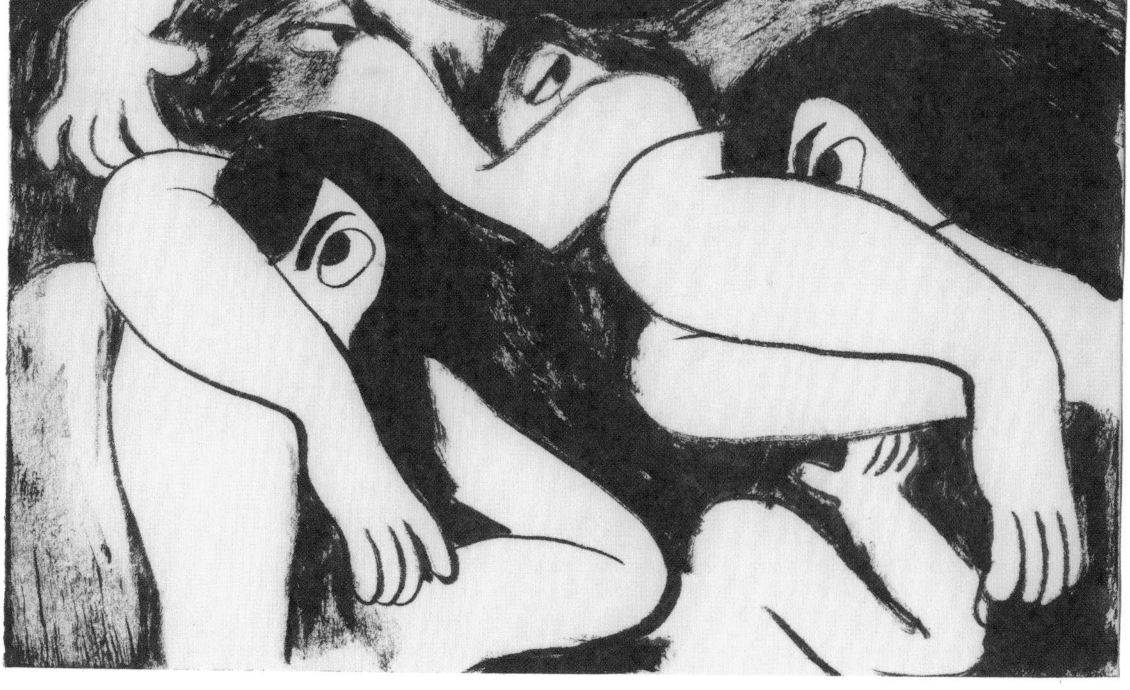

When you can't make sense of anything.

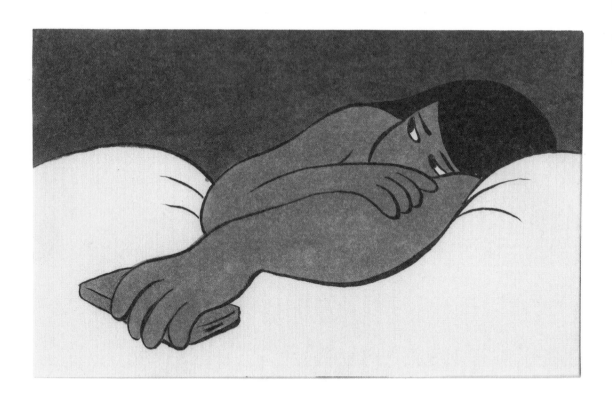

When you're painfully in love.

When nothing feels right.

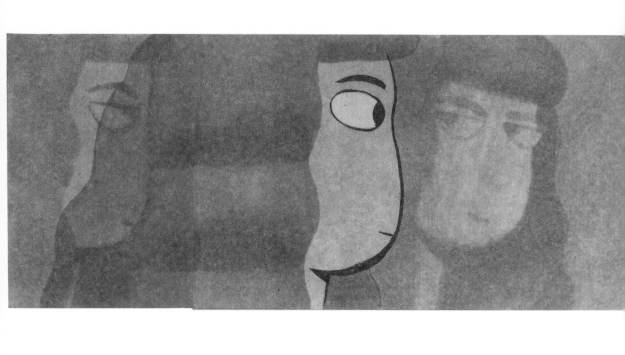

When your thoughts hold you in contempt.

When you're at an impasse.

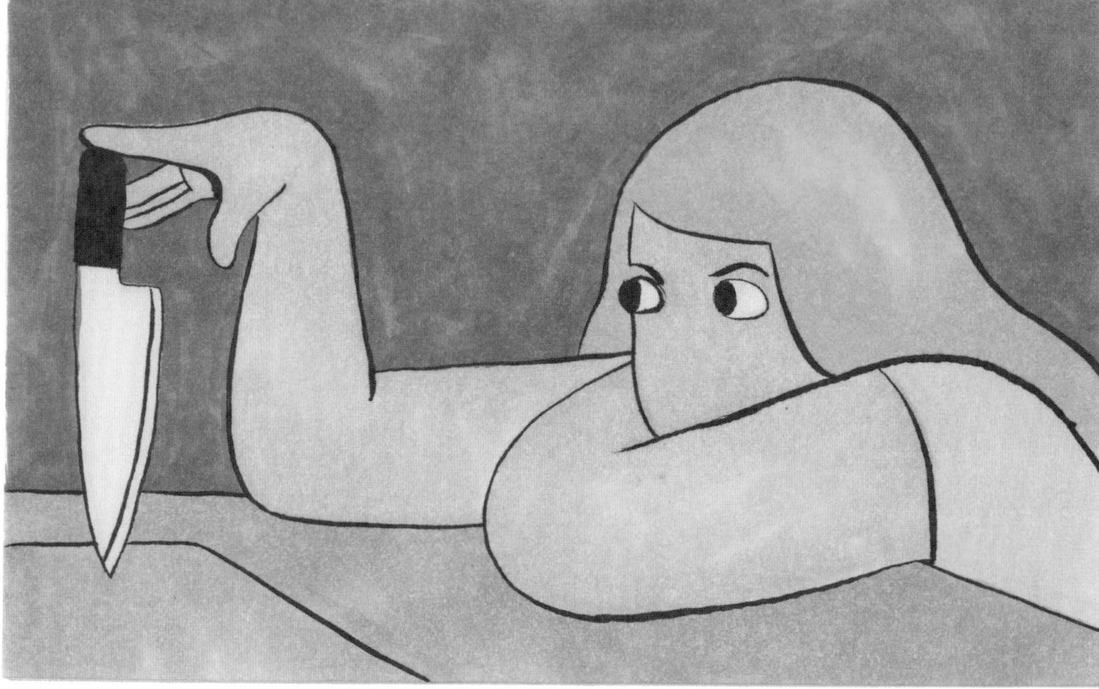

When you're about to cook him dinner
and then you start thinking about that time
he didn't compliment your haircut.

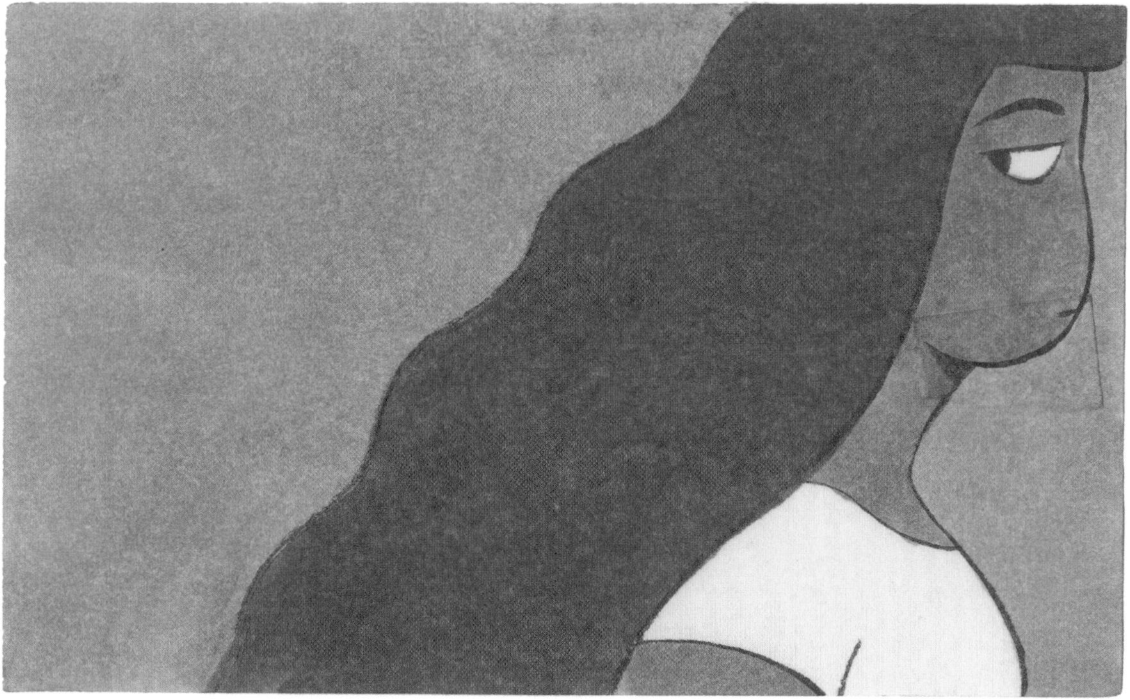

When you have doubts.

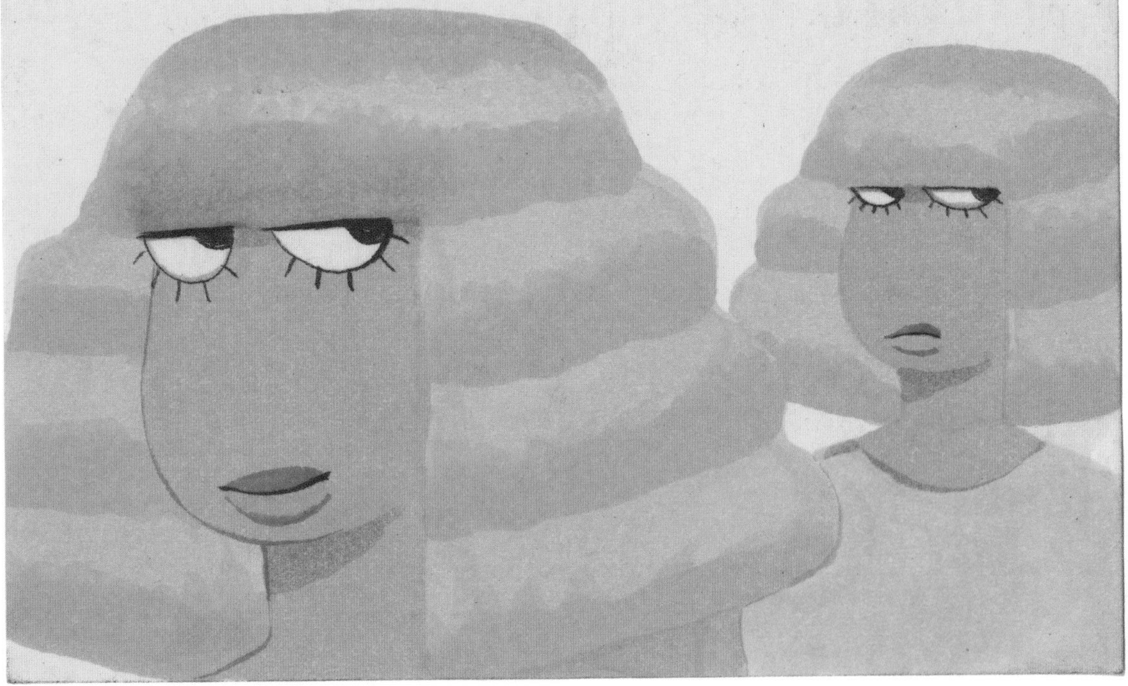

When someone you don't like tells a funny joke
but you still don't like them.

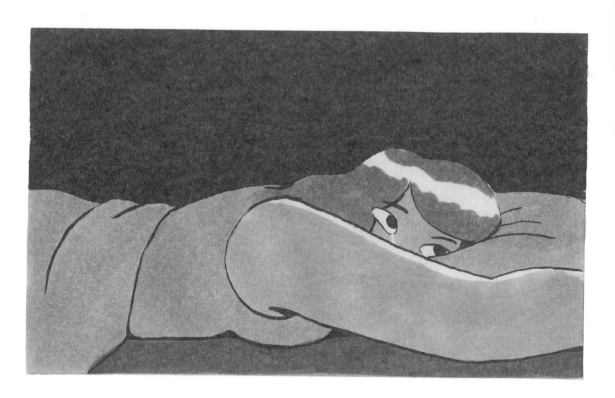

When it used to be the amazing sex
that wore you out but now he exhausts you
without even touching you.

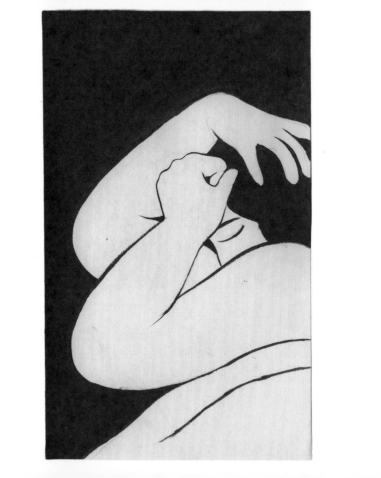

When loneliness arrives in its most
sadistic form at night.

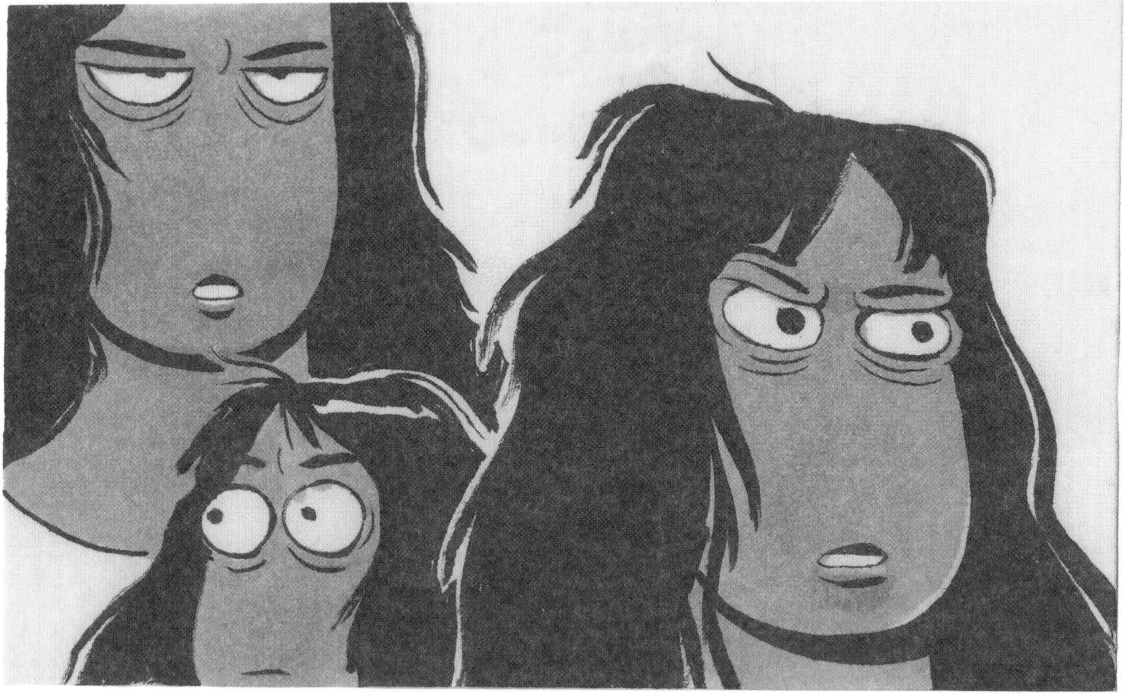

When you've been alone with your thoughts for too long.

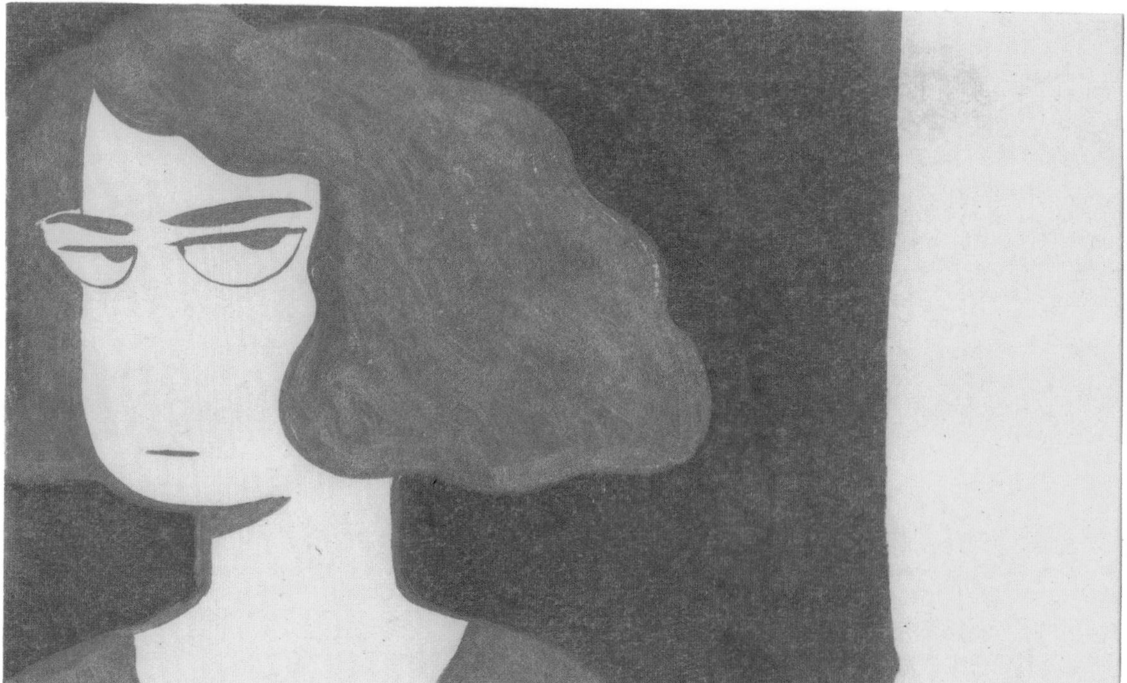

When you always brace yourself for heartbreak
so you never get close to anyone.

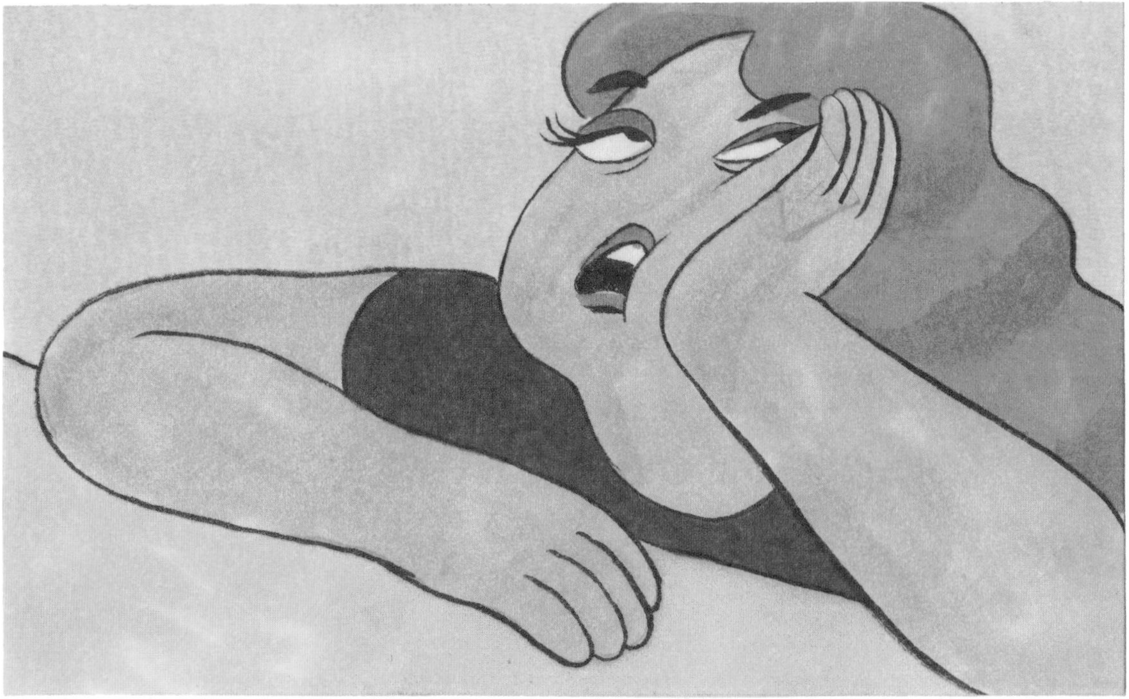

When you're exhausted from
a day full of over-thinking.

CHAPTER 4

ADORATION UNENCUMBERED BY REASON

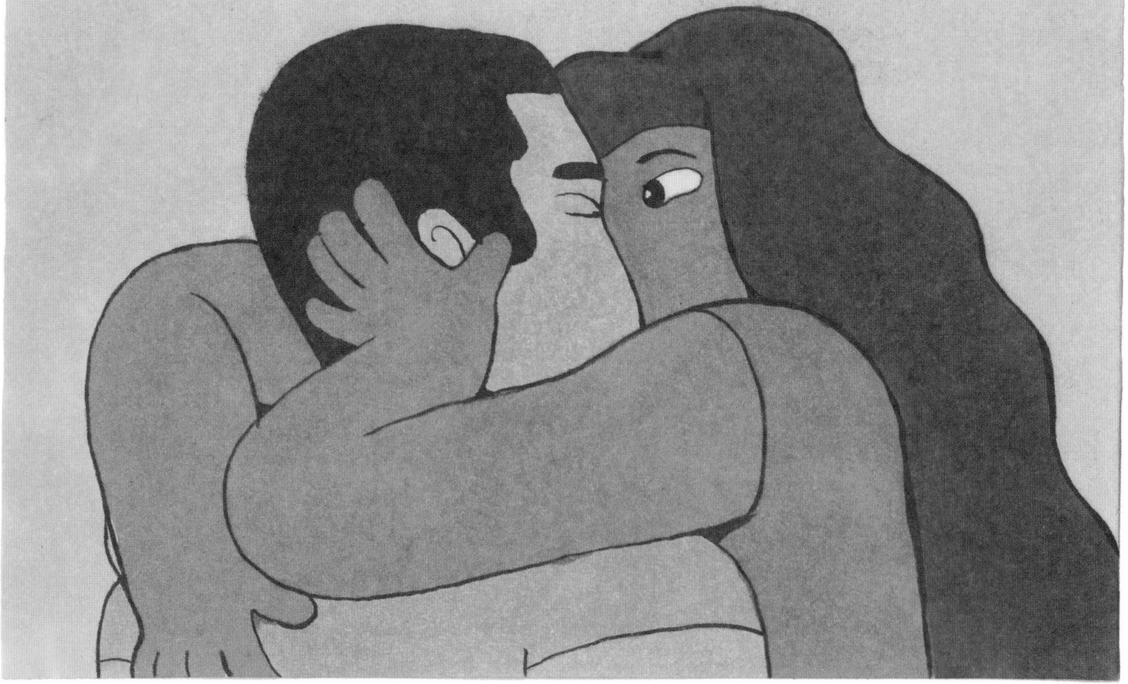

When the tension is unbearable.

When the rest of the world doesn't exist.

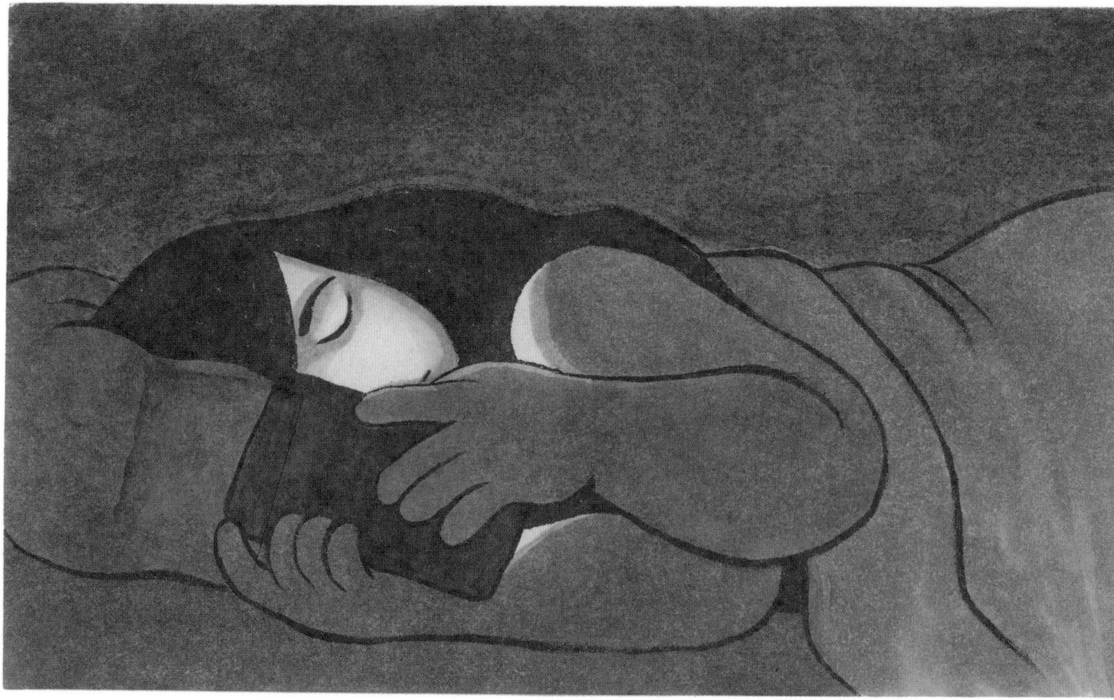

When you fall asleep texting because saying goodnight is too hard.

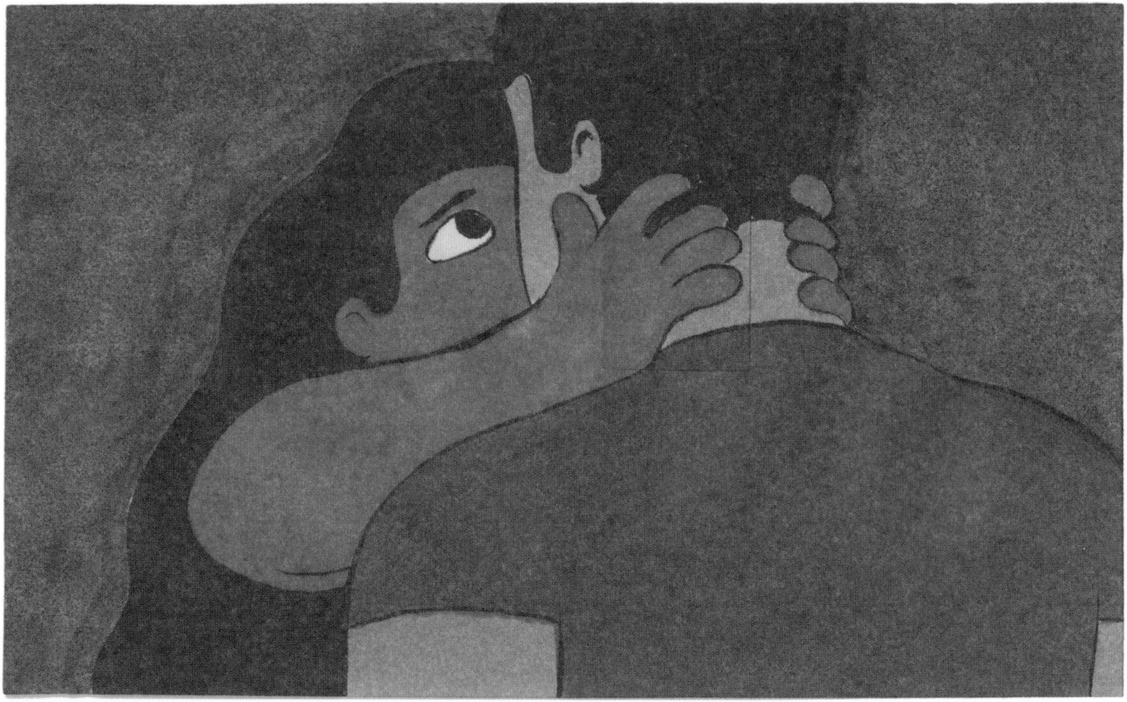

When you're searching for something that isn't there.

When you're distracted.

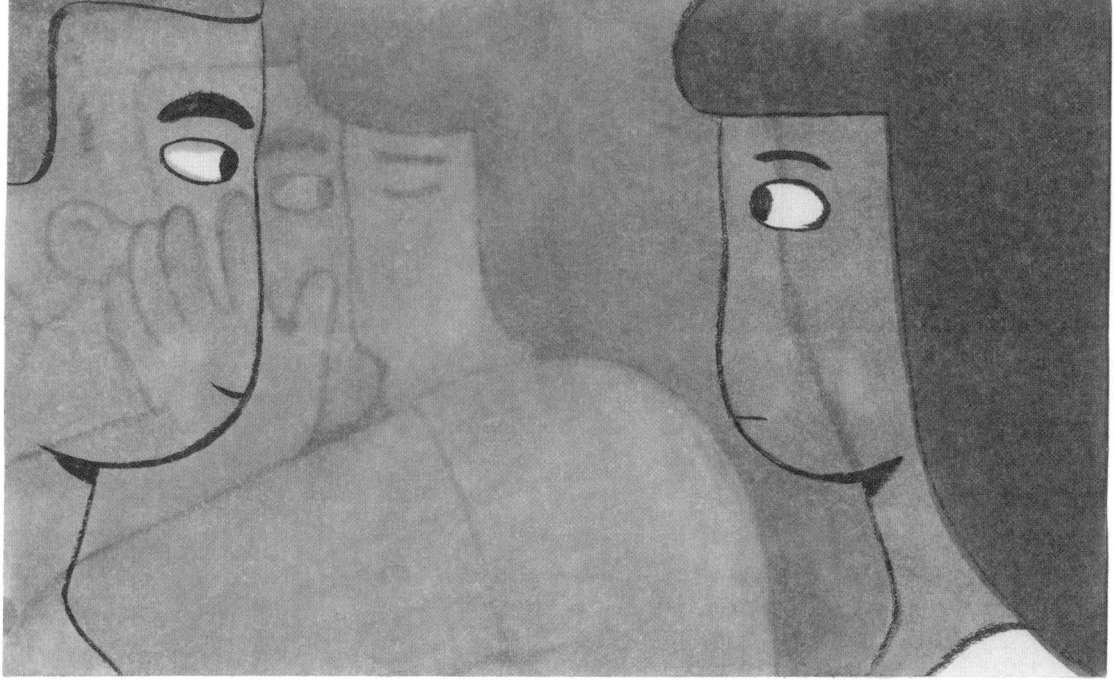

When looking at him is a form of torture
you subject yourself to willingly.

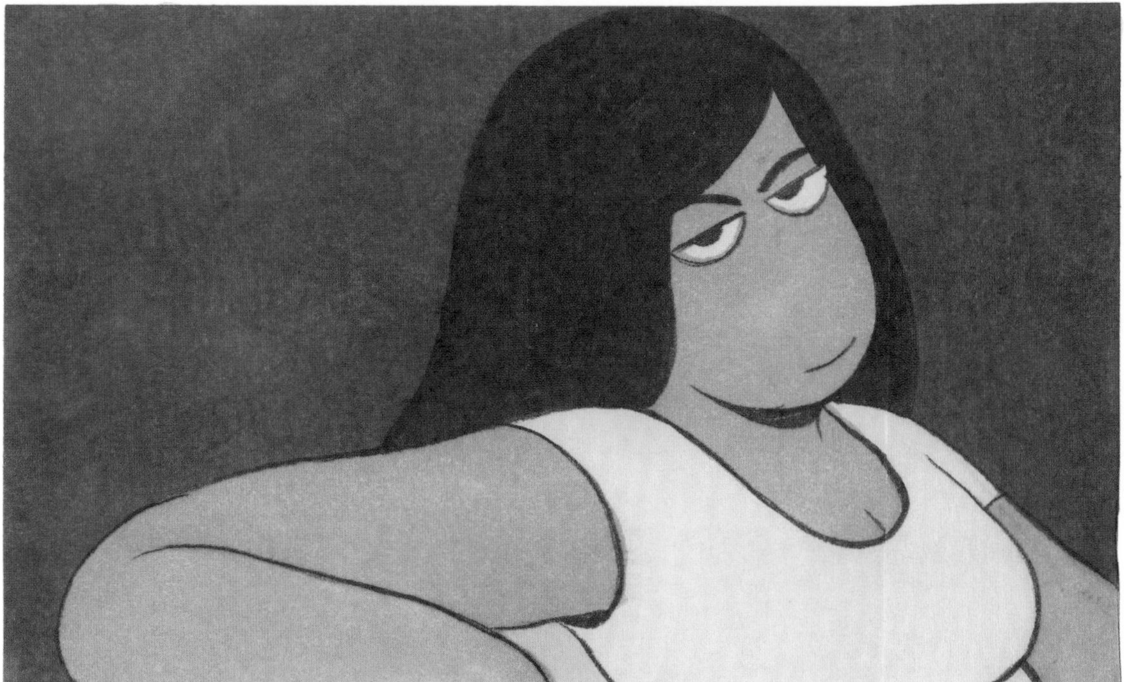

When he asks if that seat's taken
and you were already saving it for him.

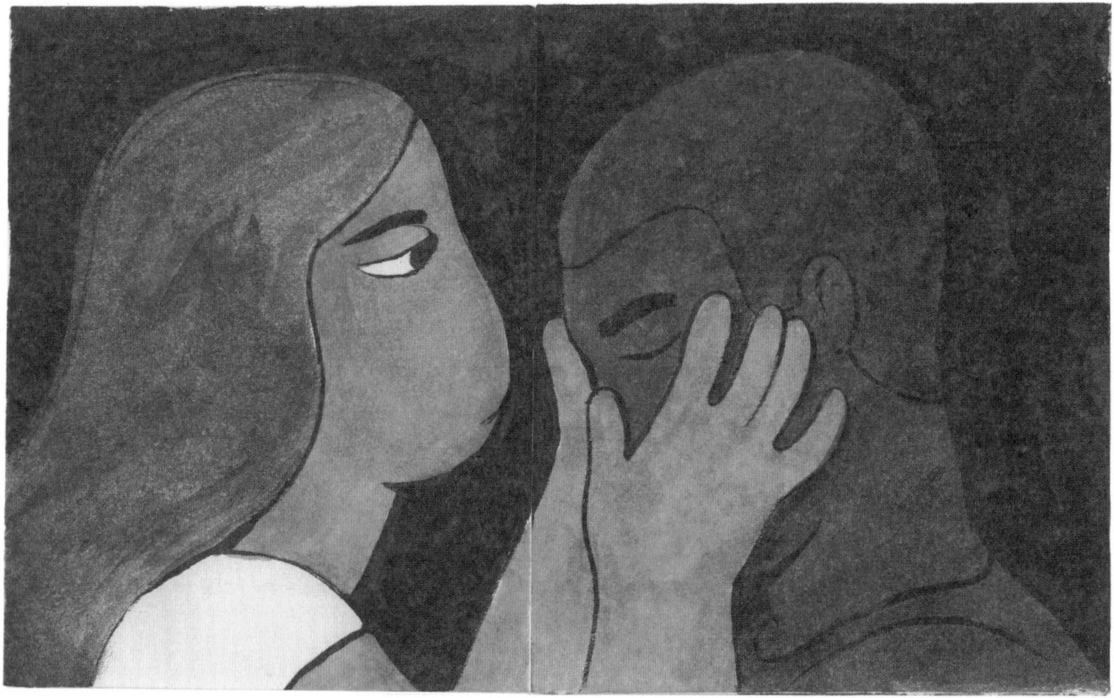

When you're wasting your breath.

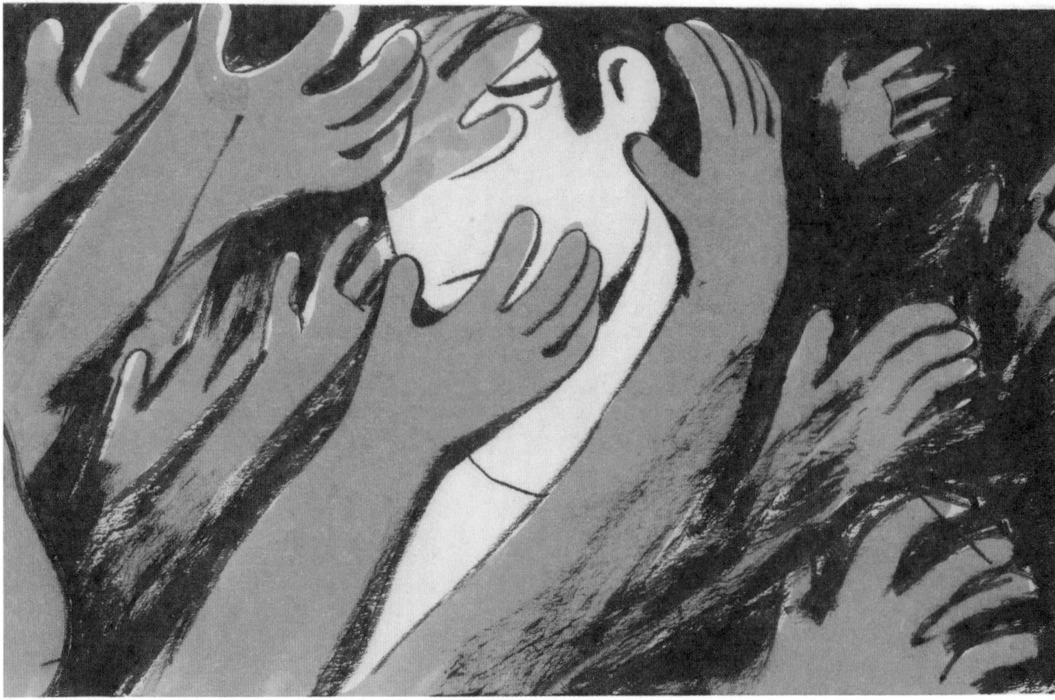

When you reach too hard.

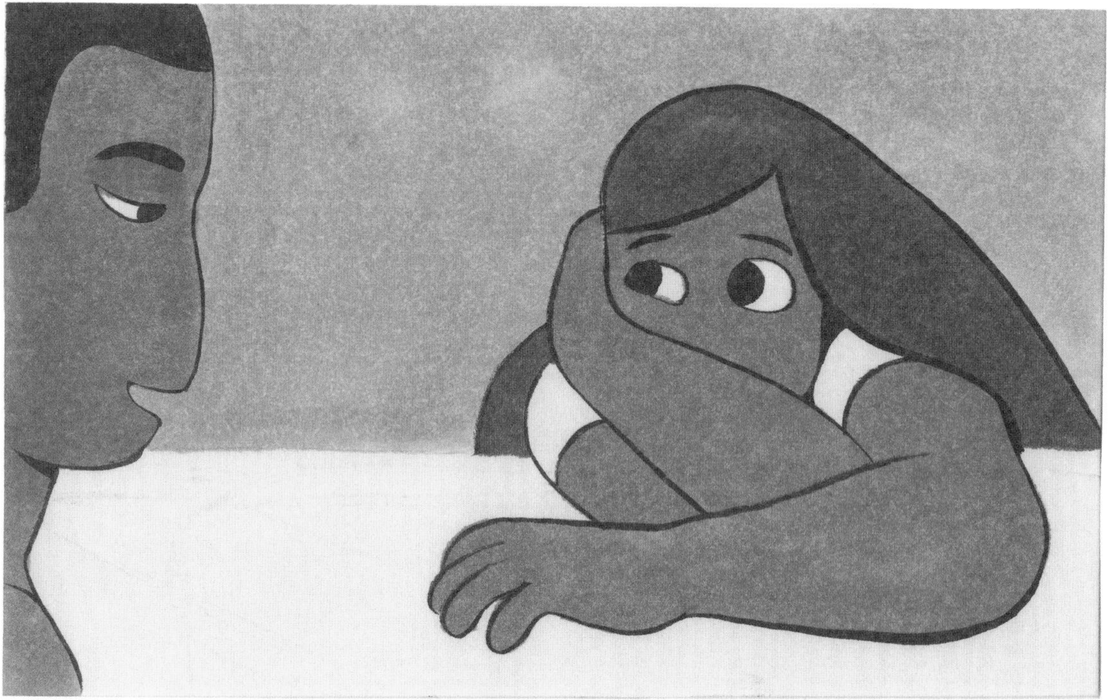

When he's telling you a story you can't understand
because he's next to you and you forgot
how to breathe or blink and unlearned your
entire vocabulary because he looked at you.

When it becomes more than lust.

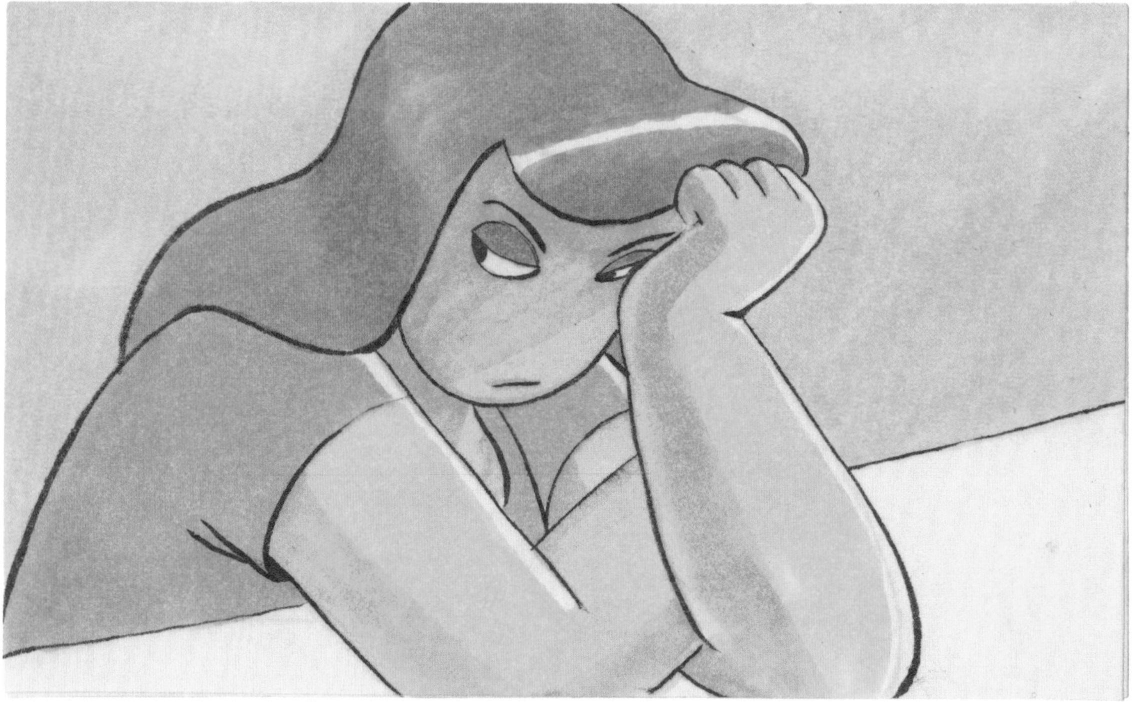

When you get caught up in your emotions.

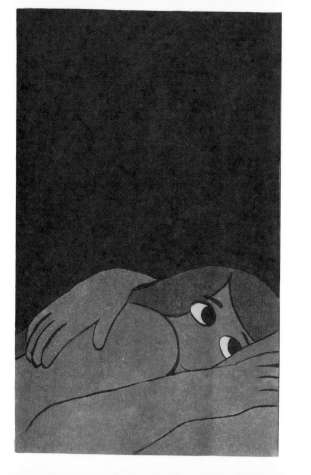

When there's no part of you that doesn't adore him.

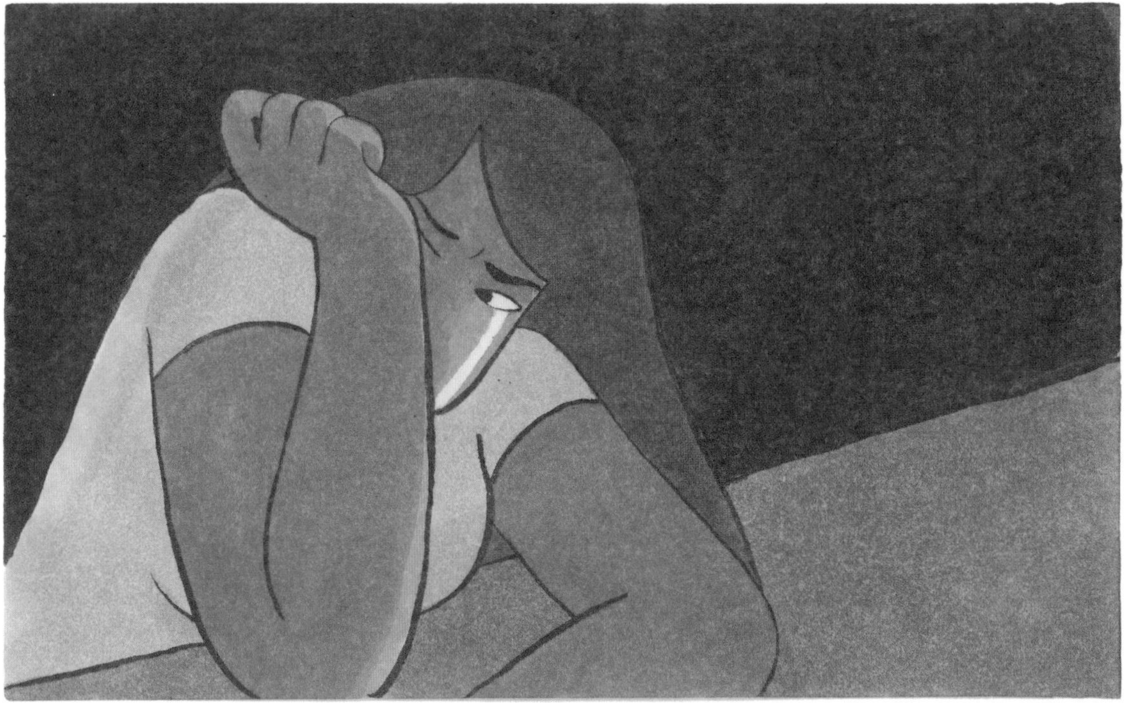

When you hurt.

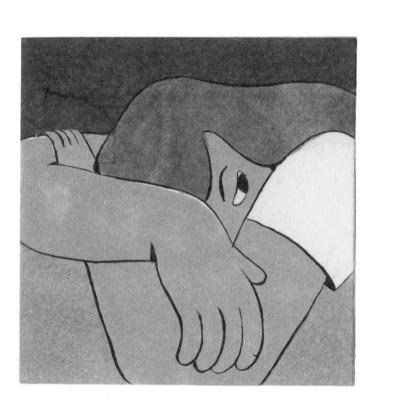

When the day allows too much time for ruminating.

When there's no resolution.

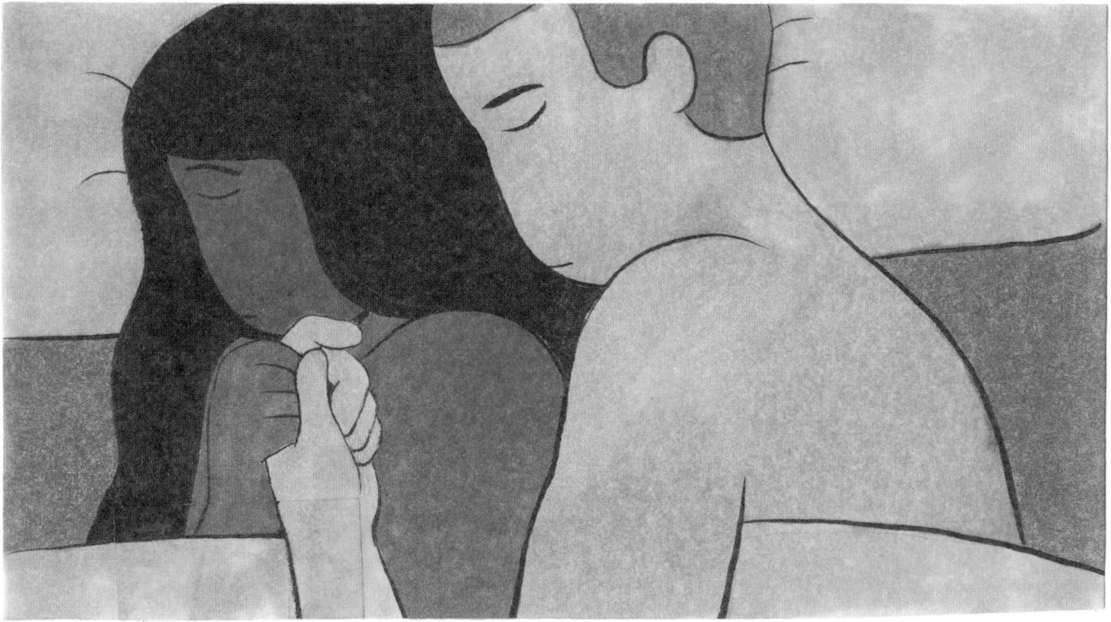

When he held your hand one night
and you haven't been the same since.

CHAPTER 5

DAILY INCONVENIENCES

When you walk outside and immediately smell the bullshit wafting in your direction.

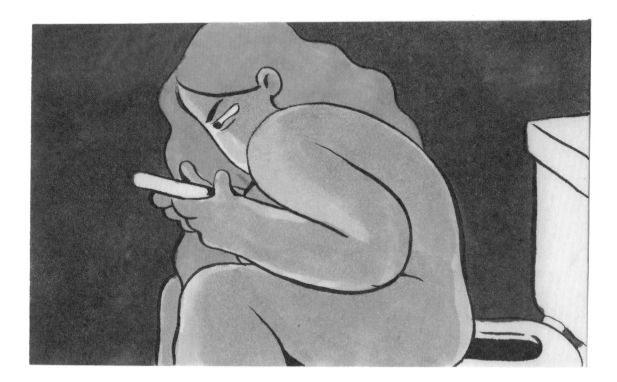

When you didn't get enough sleep and now you're searching for a playlist to wake you up during your morning poop.

When you blow on your food for a whole 45 seconds and it still burns the fuck out of your mouth.

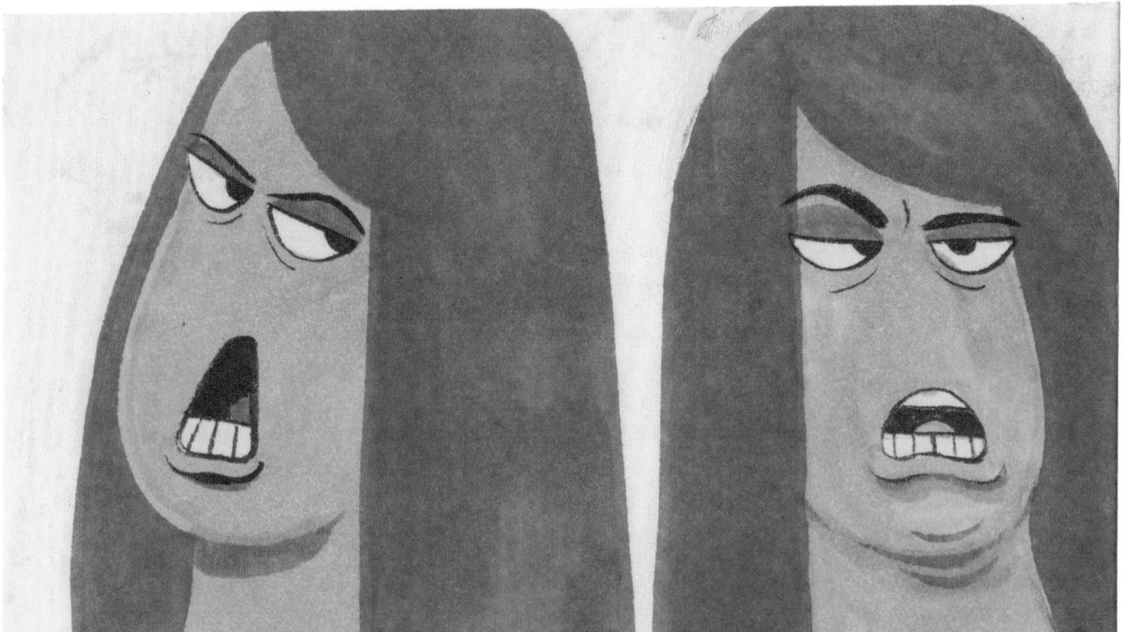

When your fucking sneeze won't come out.

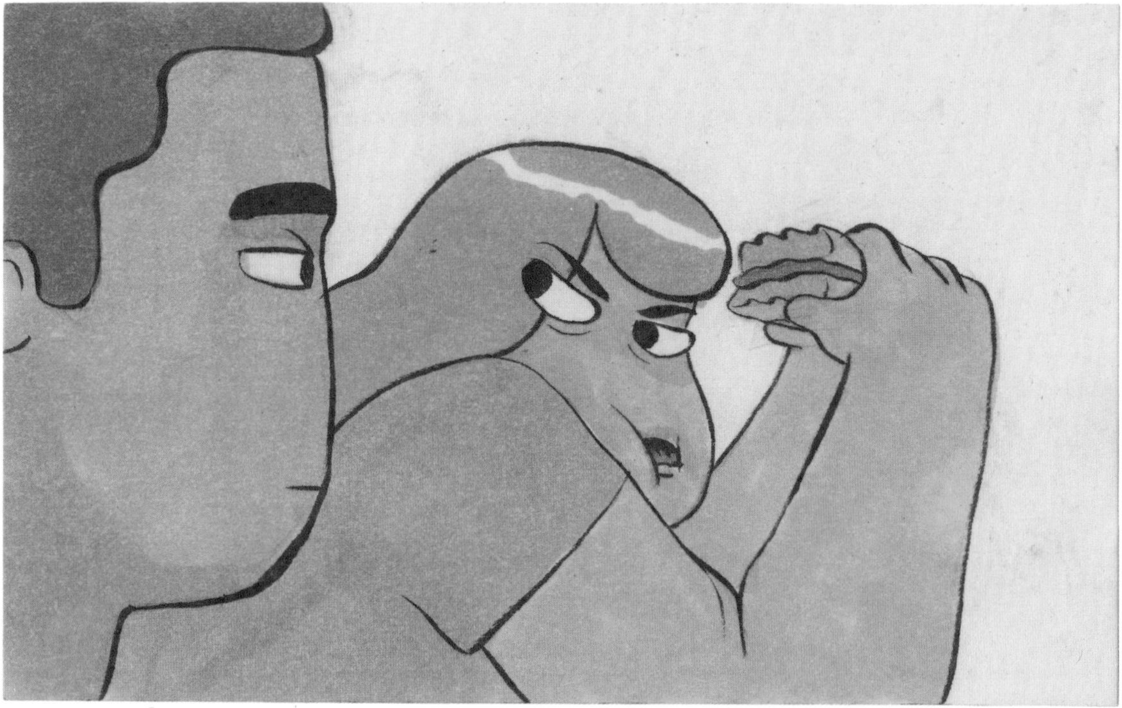

When you're in a nearly empty cafe and some asshole asks if that seat next to you is taken.

When he cries you a river for breaking up with him but has a new girlfriend 20 minutes later.

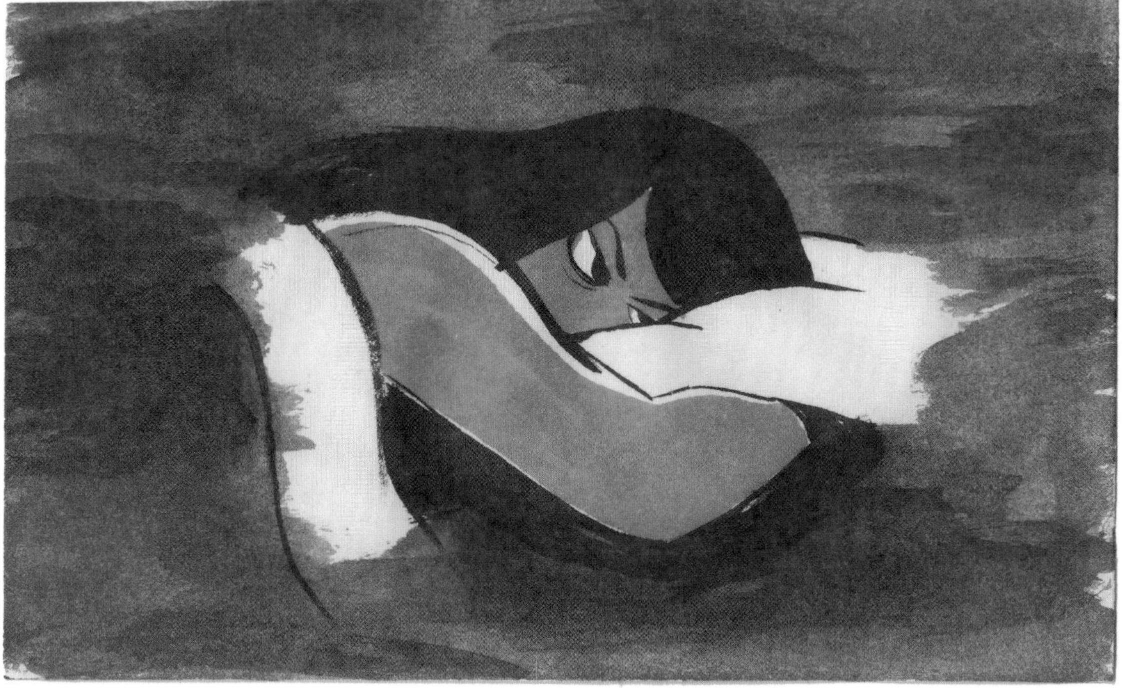

When you were having a good dream
and wake up for no reason.

When you can't appreciate anything nice
because you haven't cum for like a week.

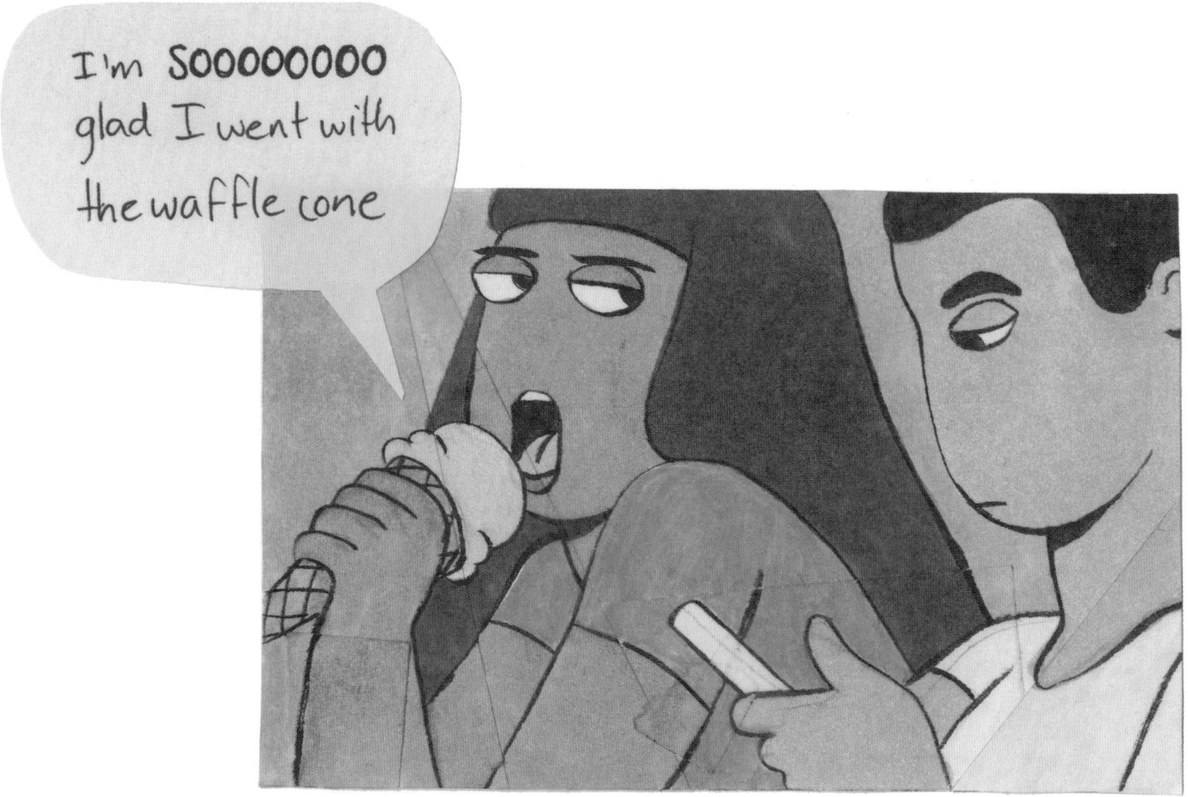
I'm SOOOOOOOO glad I went with the waffle cone

When your crush isn't paying attention to you.

When you can't decide if you want french fries
or dick.

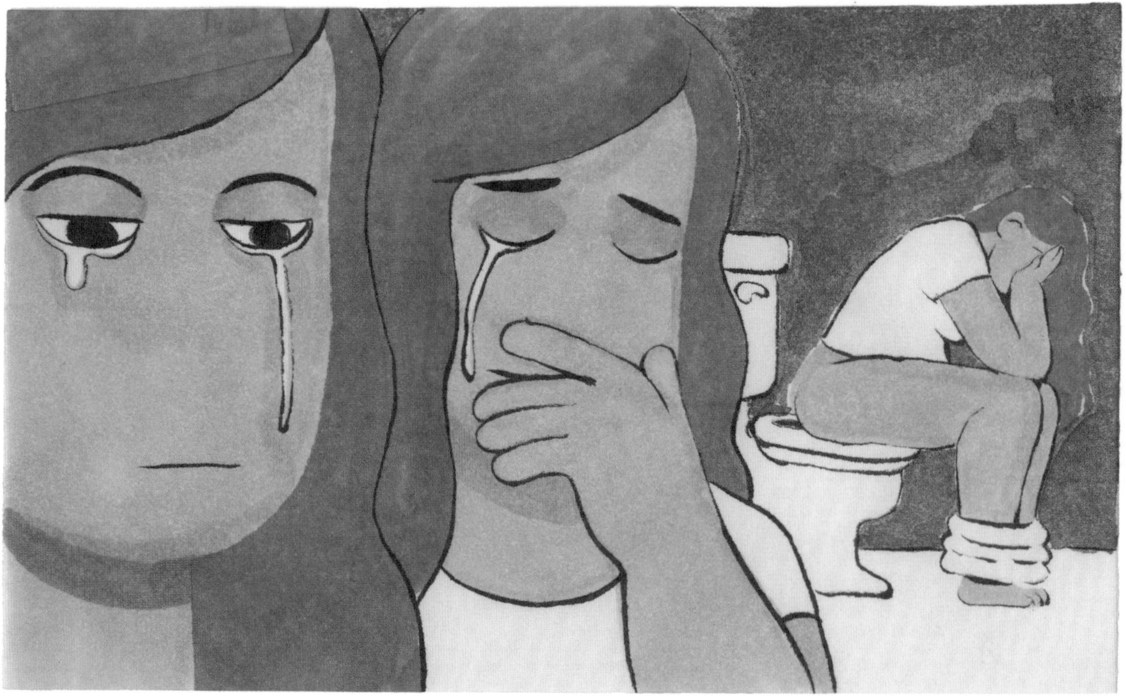

When that giant shit you excitedly ran to the toilet for is just a fart.

When the car behind you honked the moment the light turned green so you accelerate slower than usual.

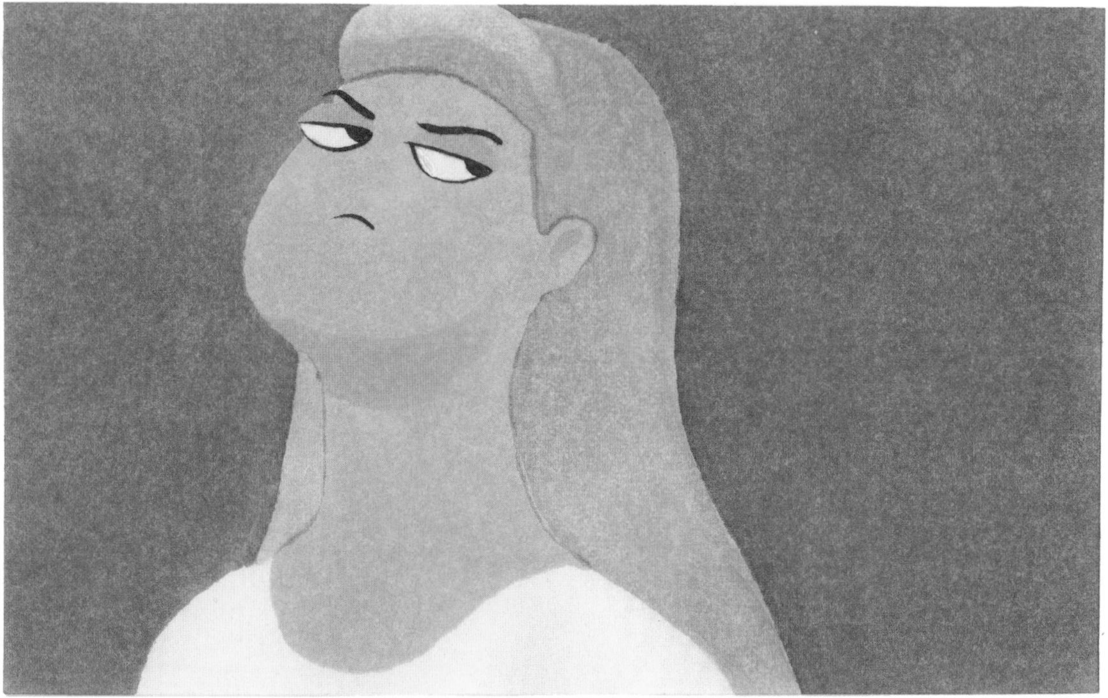

When your friend promised there would be food at the party so you skipped dinner but there isn't one fucking charcuterie board in sight.

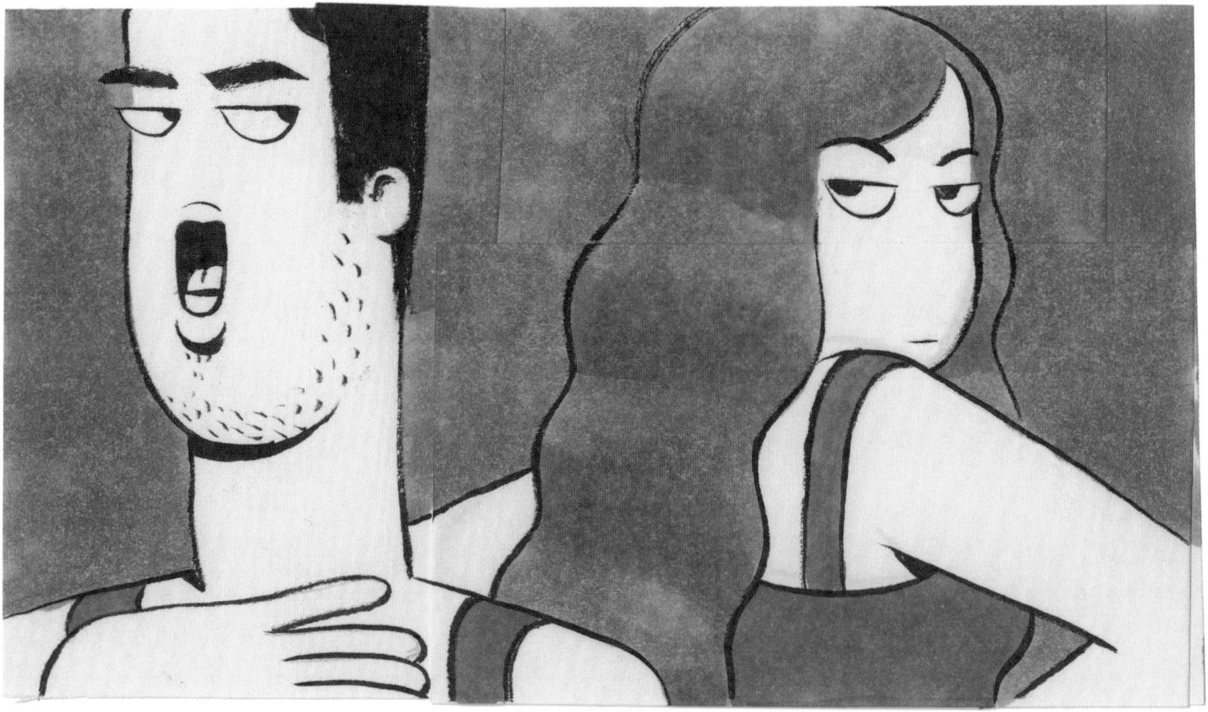

When that bitch shows up wearing the same fucking dress as you.

When you hear another girl laughing at your crush's jokes that aren't even funny.

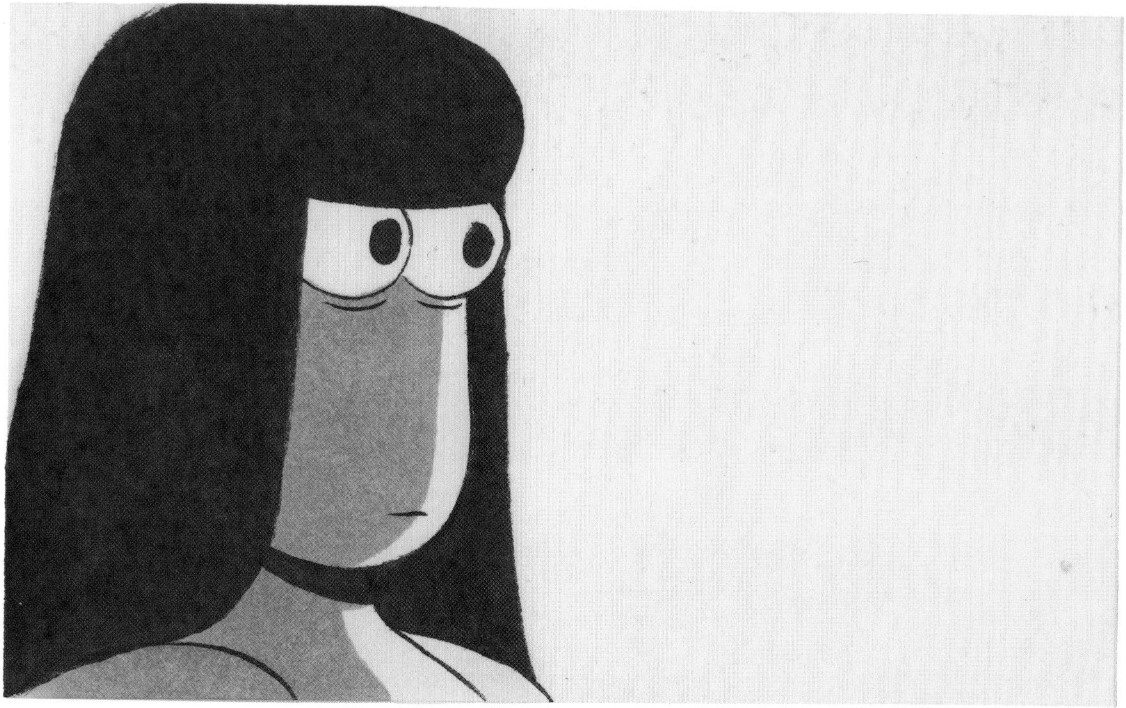

When you have the bubble guts.

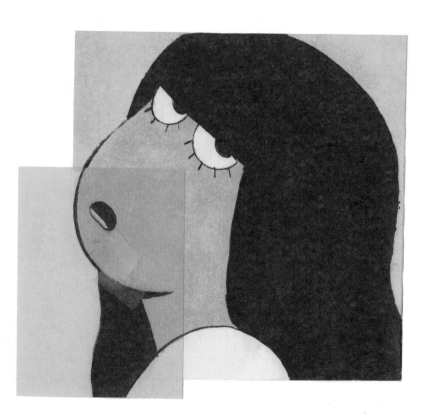

When your item shipped three fucking minutes ago and there's still no tracking number.

When your vibrators just aren't doing it for you.

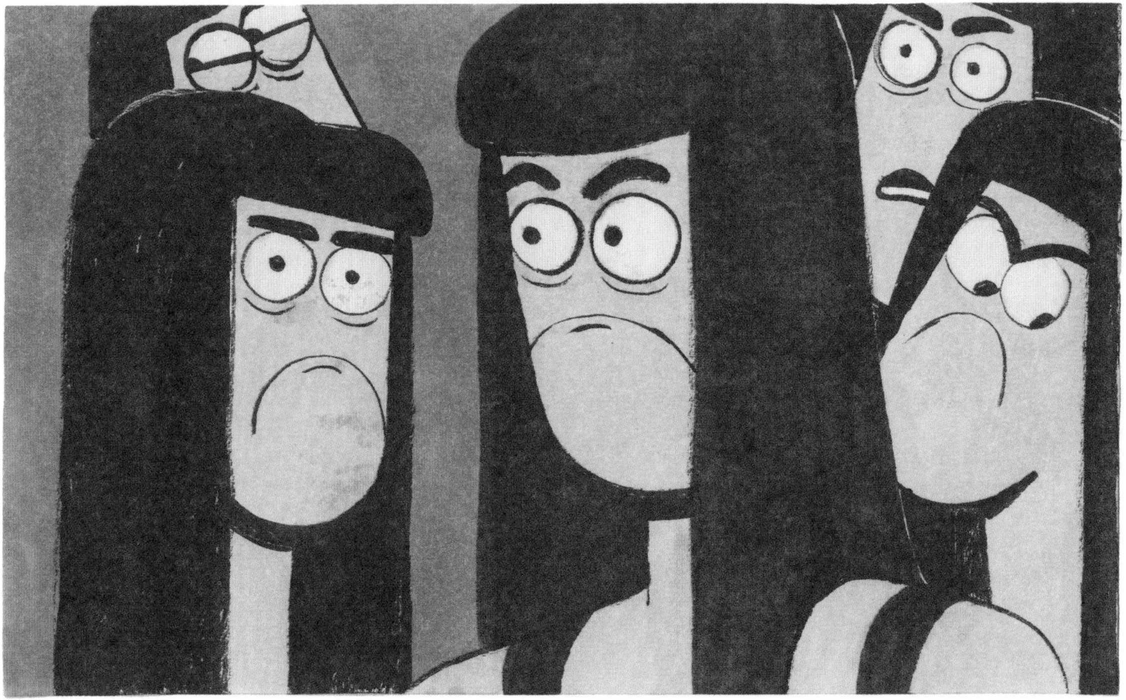

When you're about to snap.

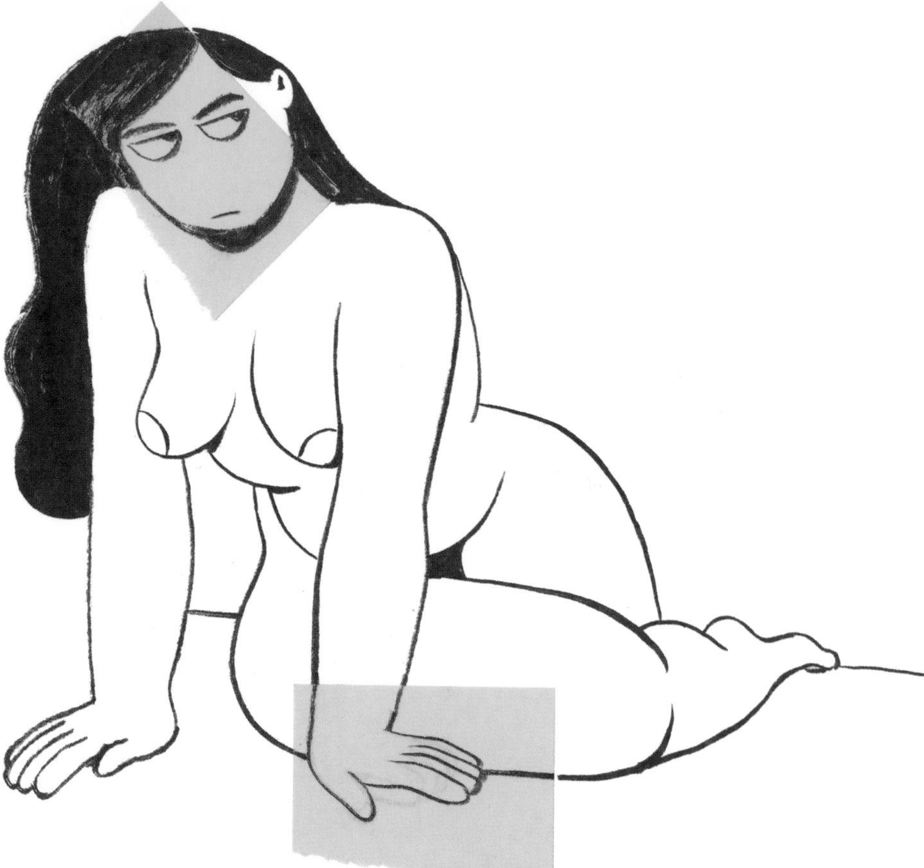

When you're thinking about canceling the dick appointment to have a nap instead.

When there's a knock on your door right before you get in the shower.

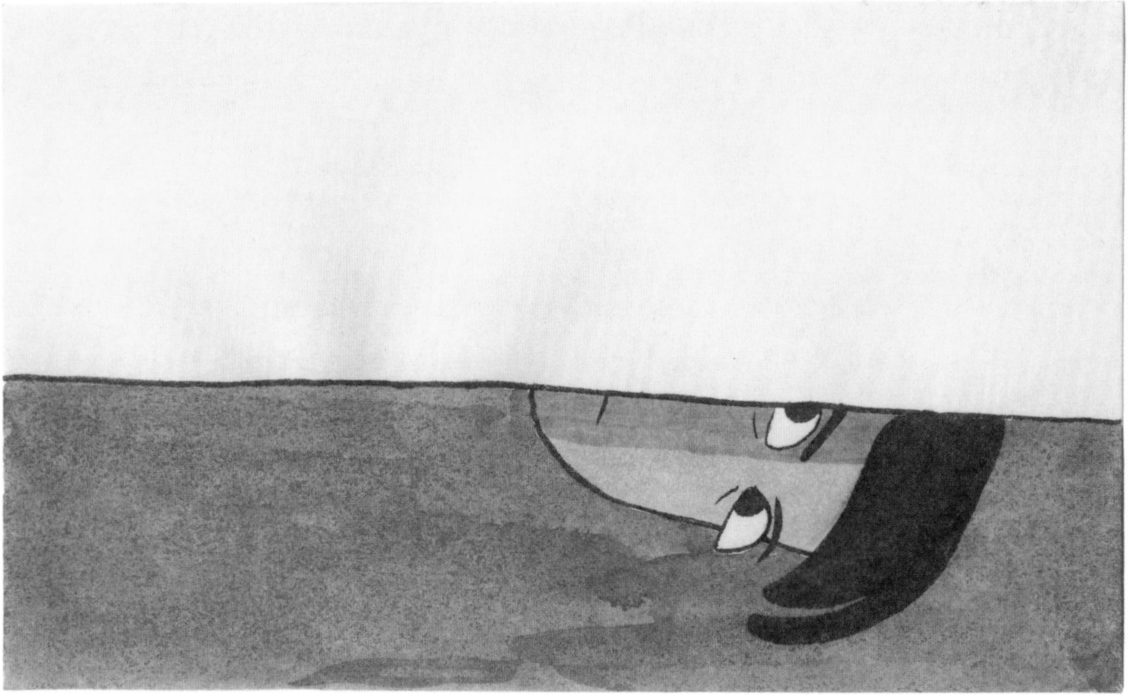

When you're in the bathroom at work, checking to make sure you can shit in peace.

When he catcalls you from inside
a moving vehicle, like a fucking pussy.

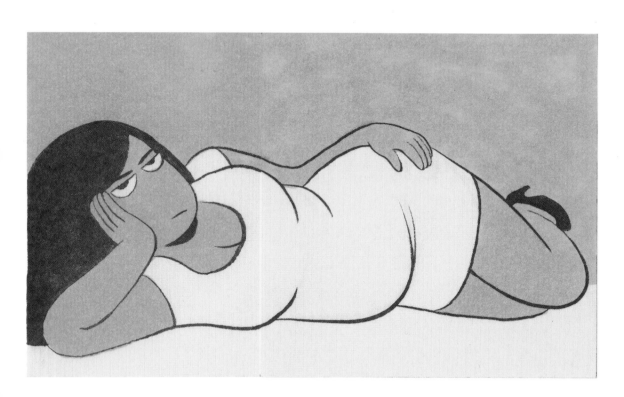

When your plans get cancelled and there's no one around to see how good you look.

When shit doesn't work in your favor.

When it's more than just a fart.

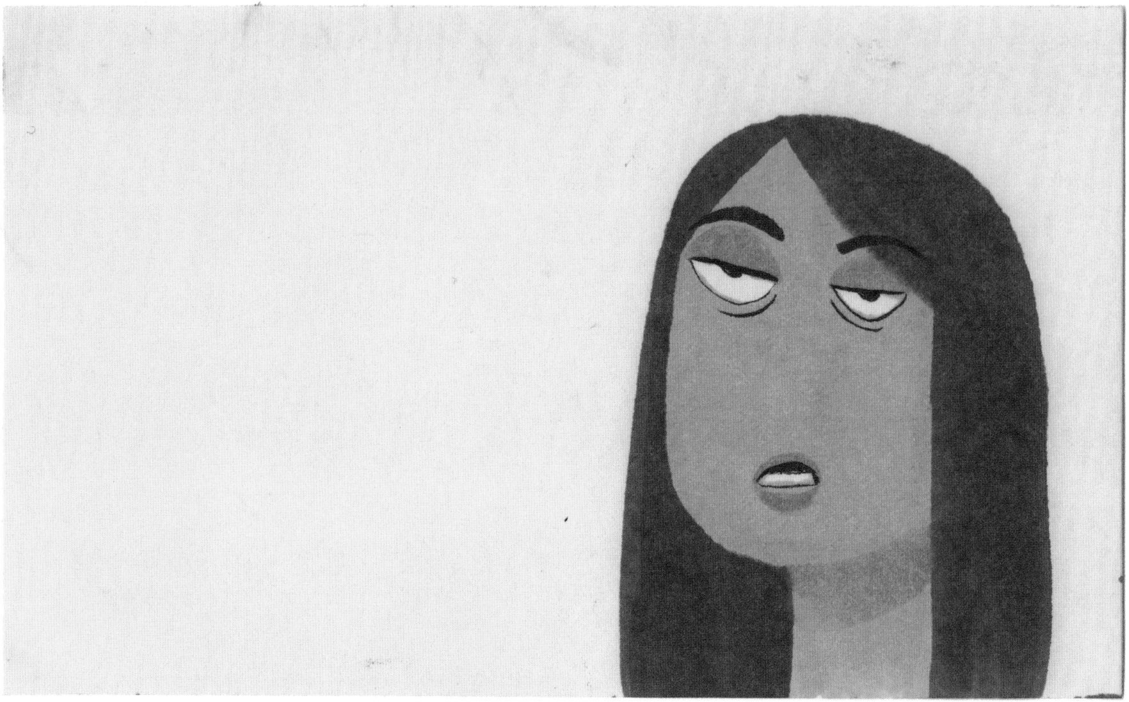

When you're just too tired for that shit.

CHAPTER 6

IF I COULD AFFORD TO LIVE WITHOUT YOU

When you're feigning outrage just to get him to apologize and you get your way.

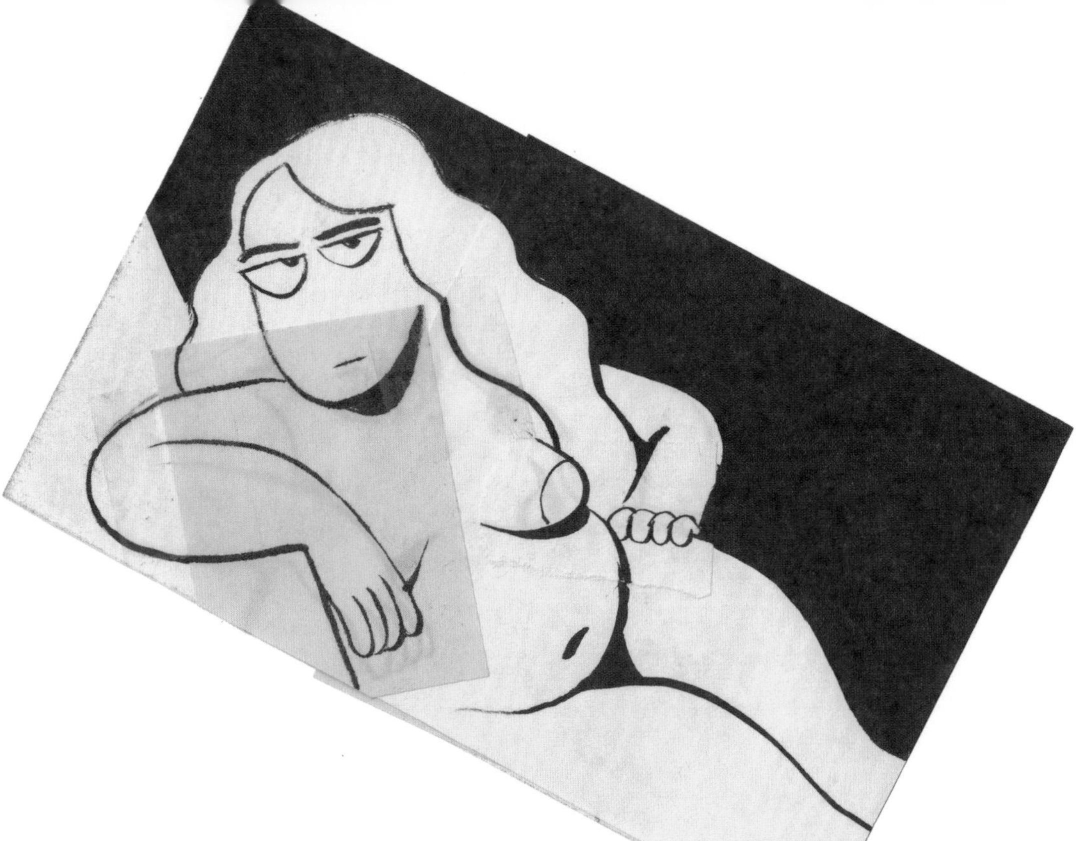

When he promised round two and now he's talking about how early he has to get up tomorrow.

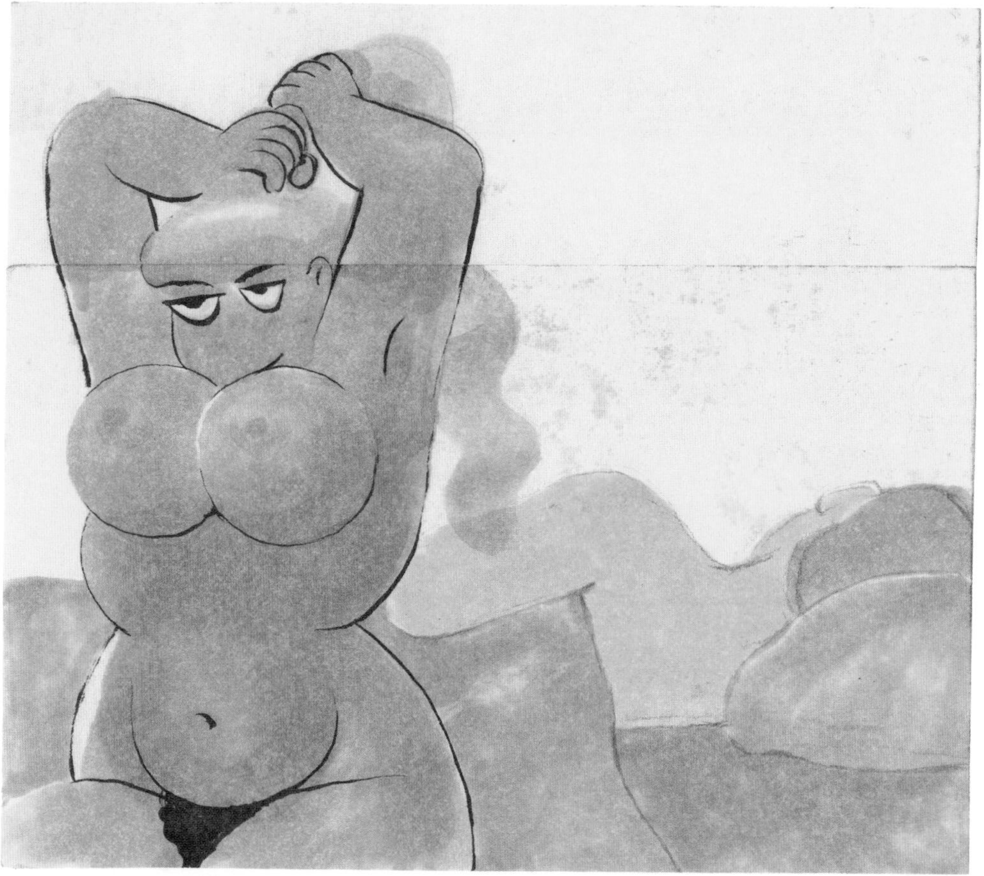

When he's not responding to your gentle kisses but you have a strategy for this kind of situation.

When the love goes away.

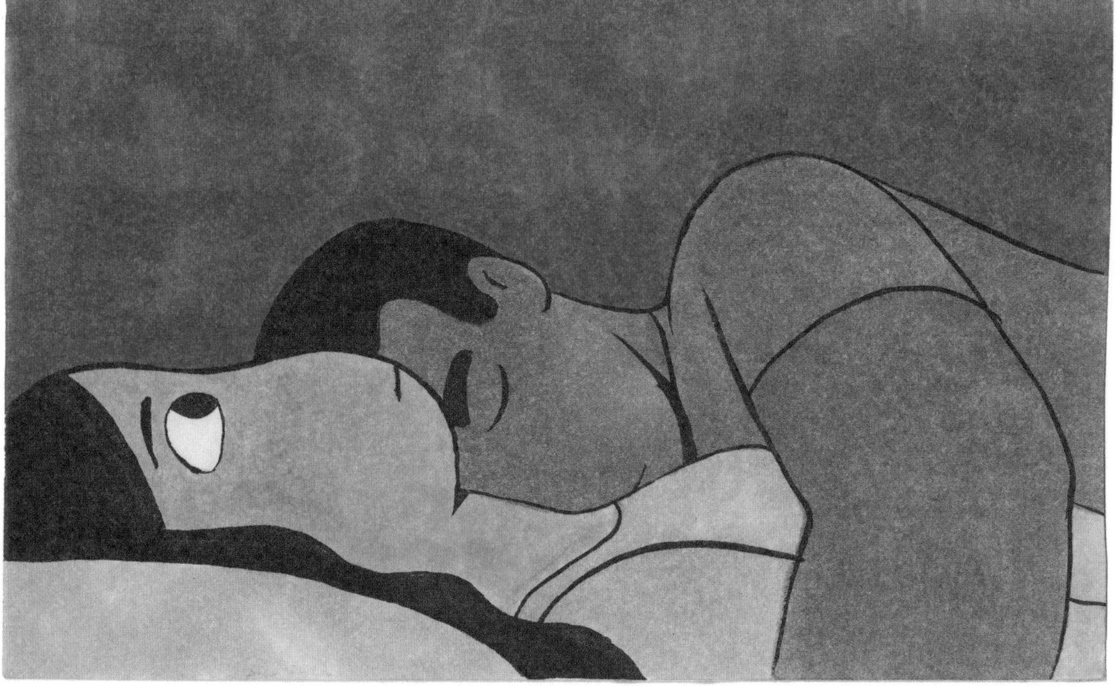

When you can't reconcile your need for independence with your fear of being alone.

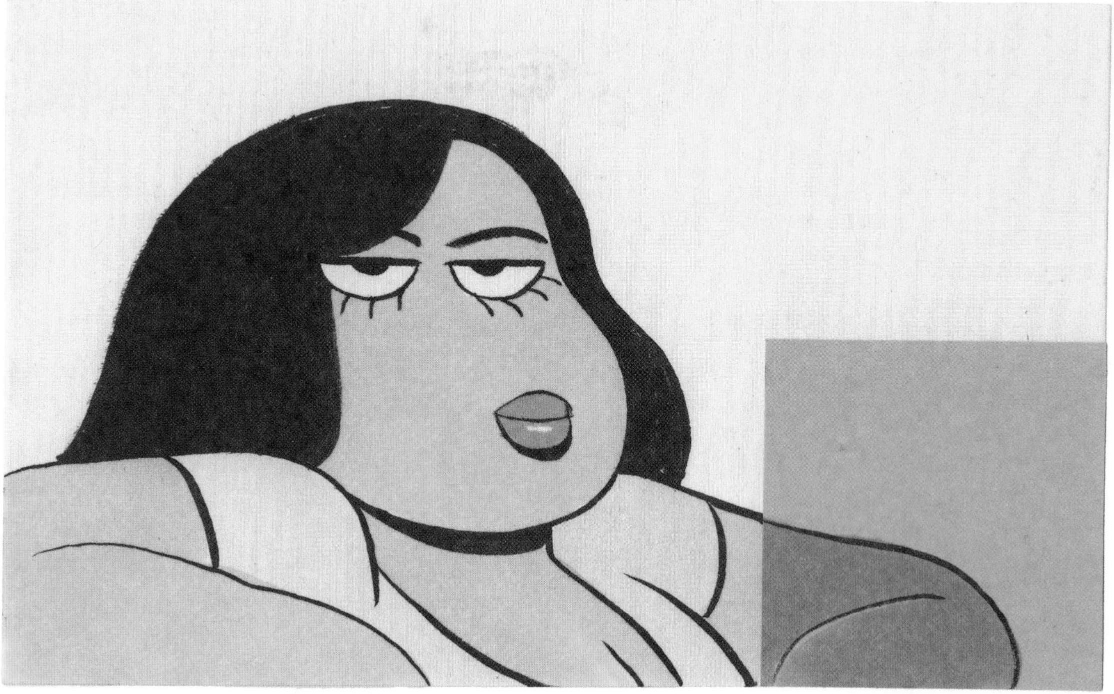

When you win an argument and now
he won't look at you.

When you're just trying to bitch about your day and he starts telling you what to do about it.

When you're tired of telling him where your clit is.

When he better fucking not.

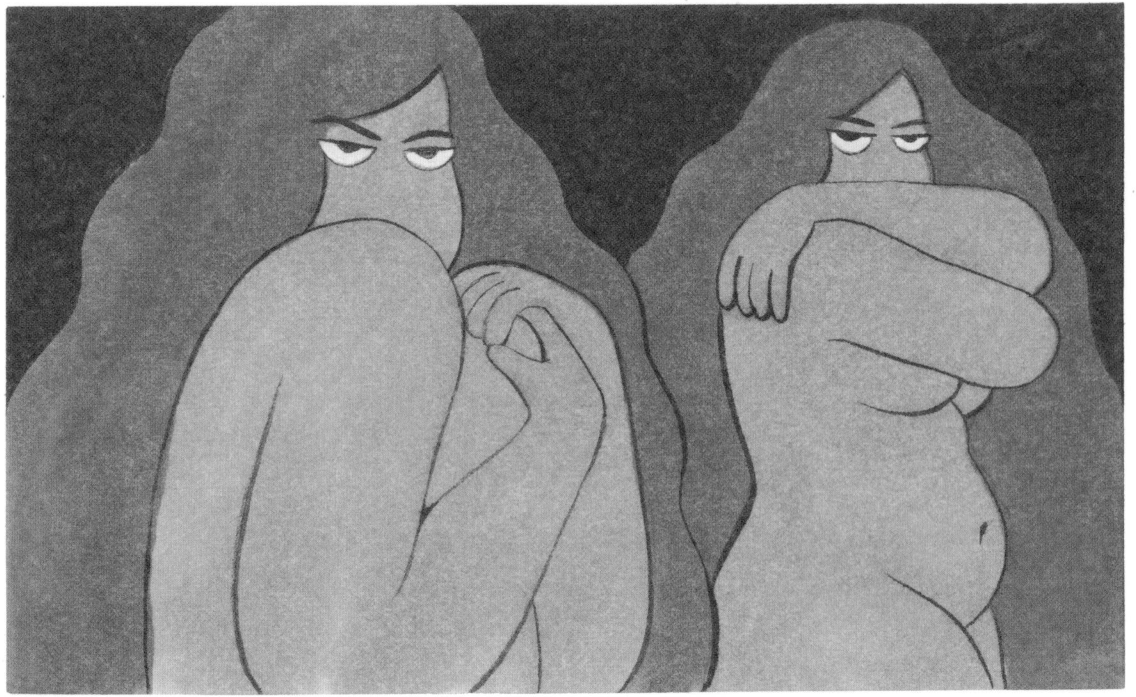

When you just had an argument and he walks
into the room while you're getting ready for bed.

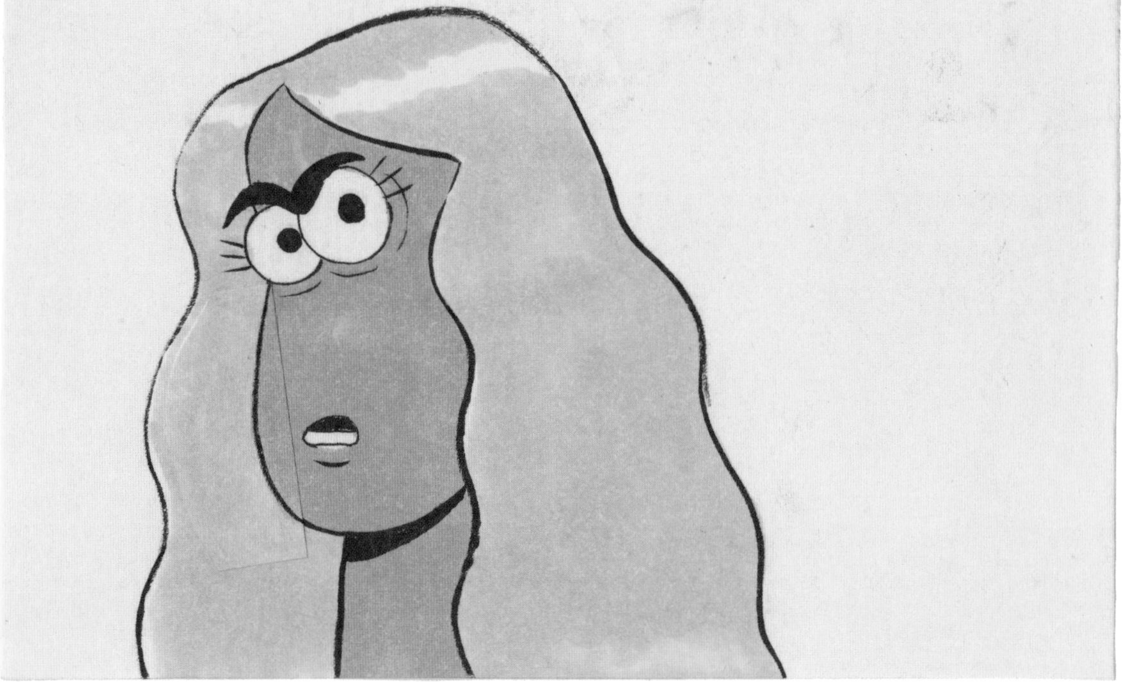

When you're gonna have a meltdown.

CHAPTER 7

UNAPOLOGETIC

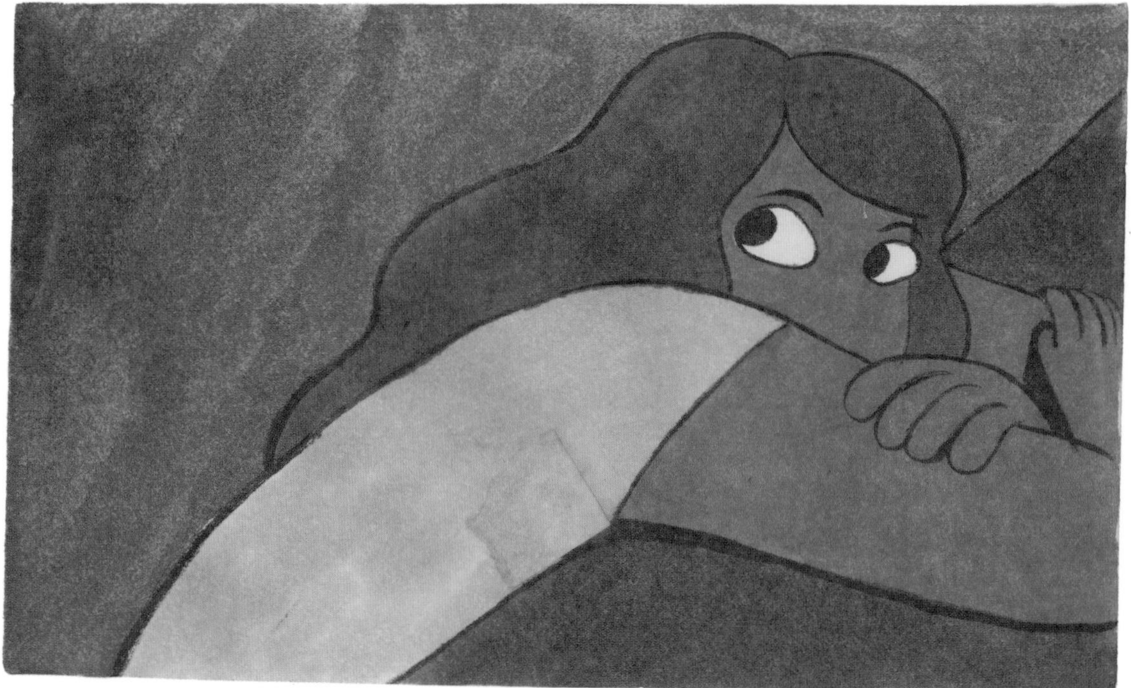

When your brooding is incessant.

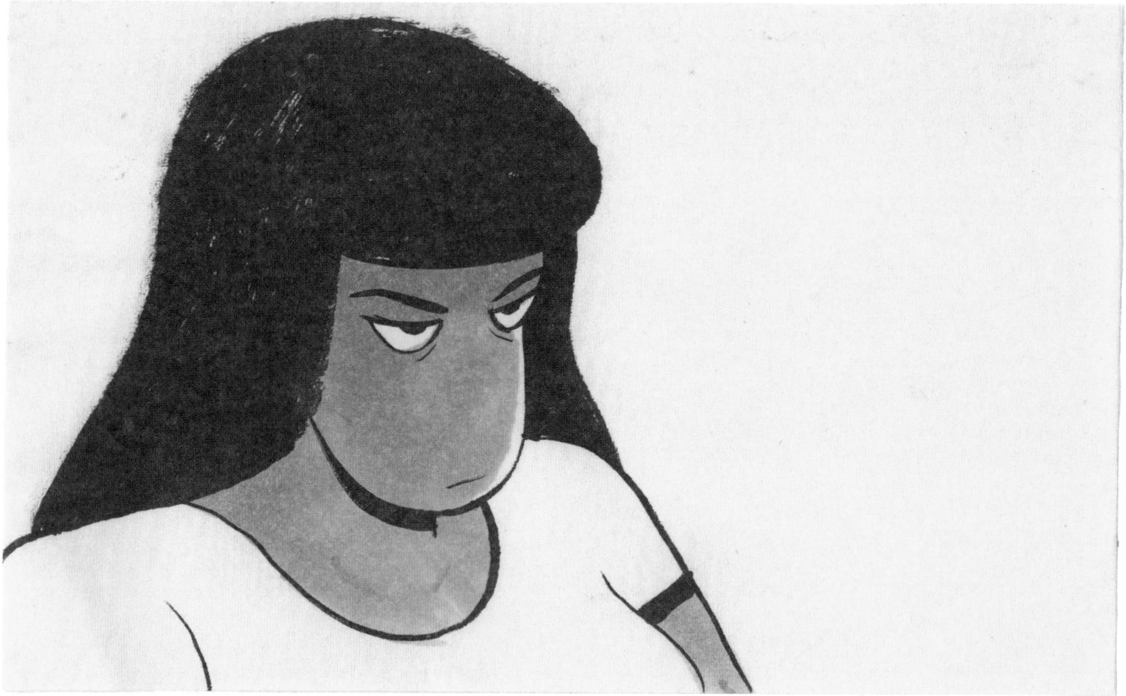

When you're not here to impress anyone.

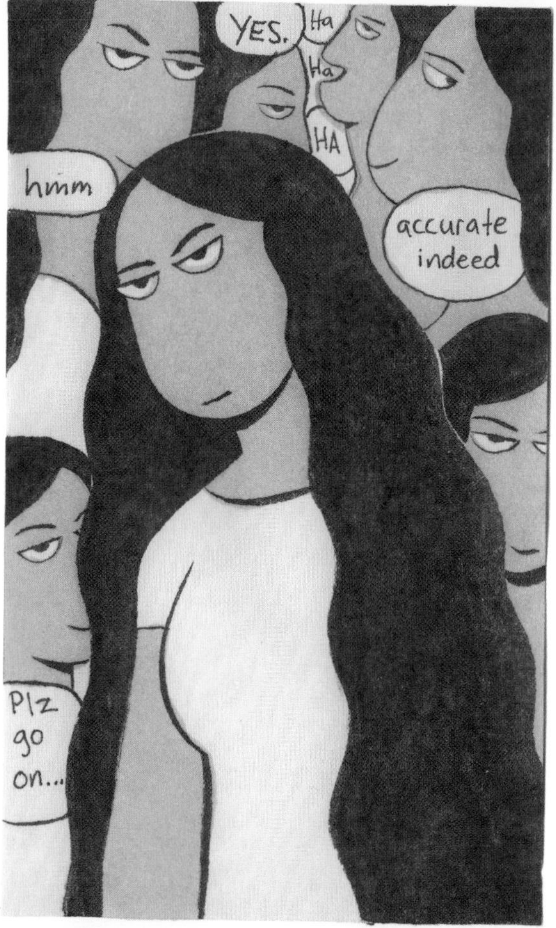
YES.
Ha
Ha
HA
hmm
accurate indeed
Plz go on...

When you hear people talking shit about you.

When you're not mad and then someone asks what's wrong, which reminds you that your neutral expression is read as hostility, so now you're pissed.

When bitterness is part of your identity.

When you go as a bitch for Halloween because it requires no preparation.

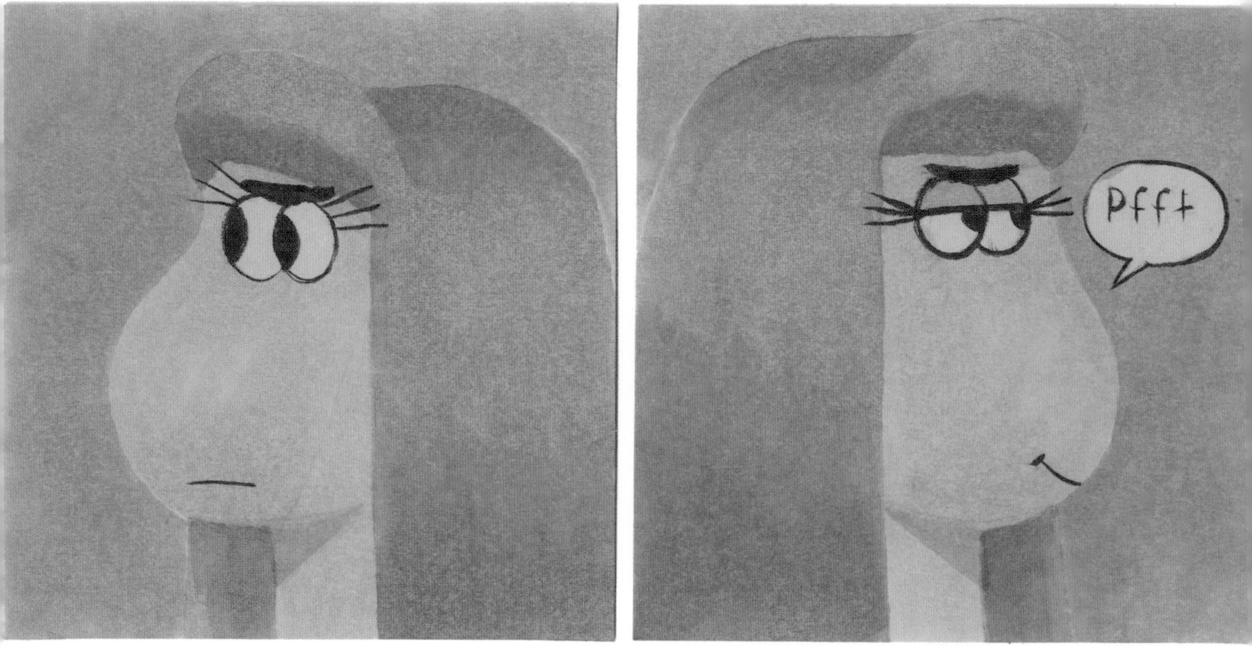
Pfft

When you see someone flirting with your crush but then you remember who the fuck you are.

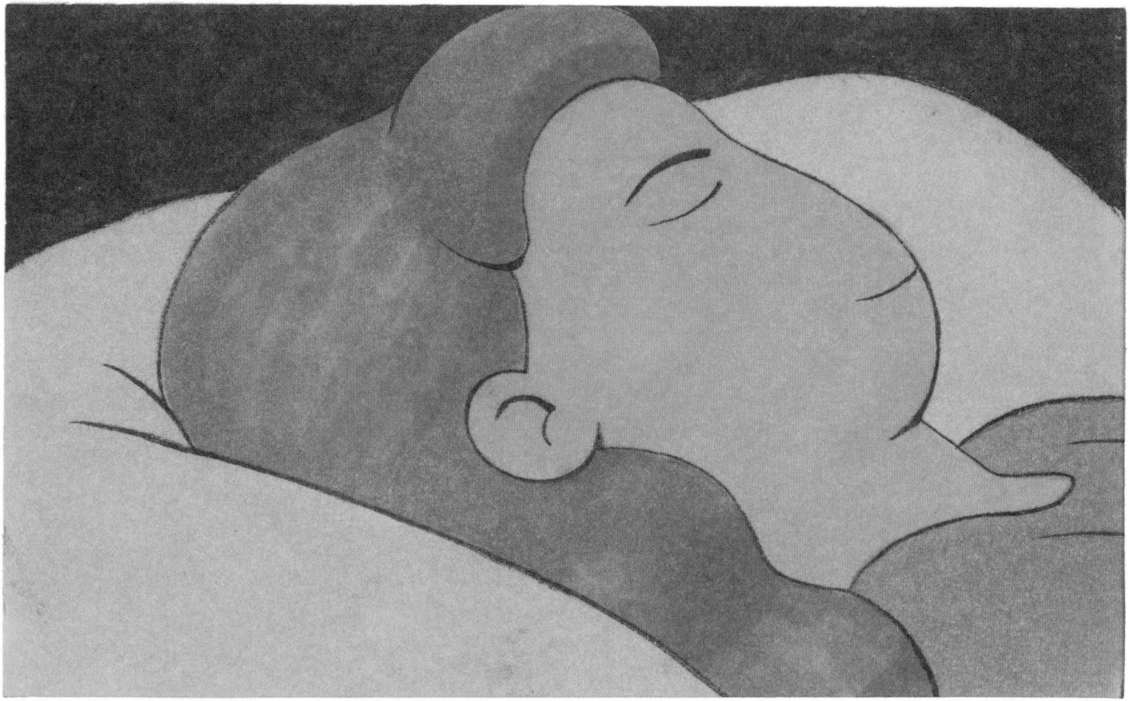

When everyone else can just fuck off.

When you're too perfect to be seen by anyone.

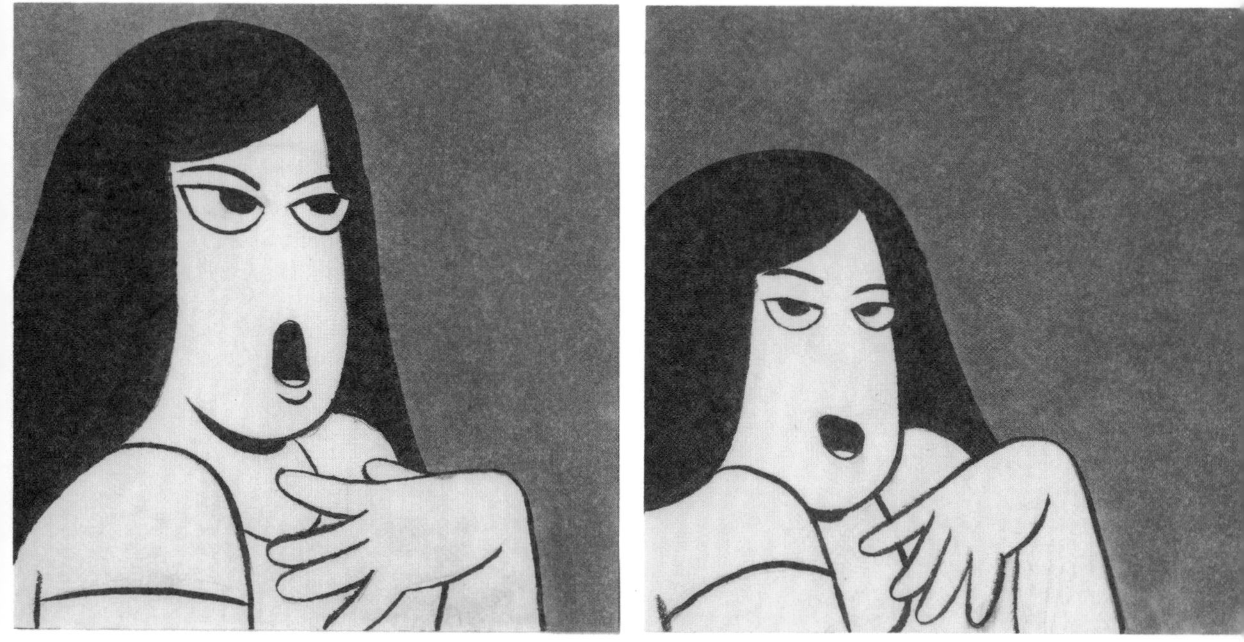

When you get accused of something you totally did.

When your angry heart navigates your whole existence.

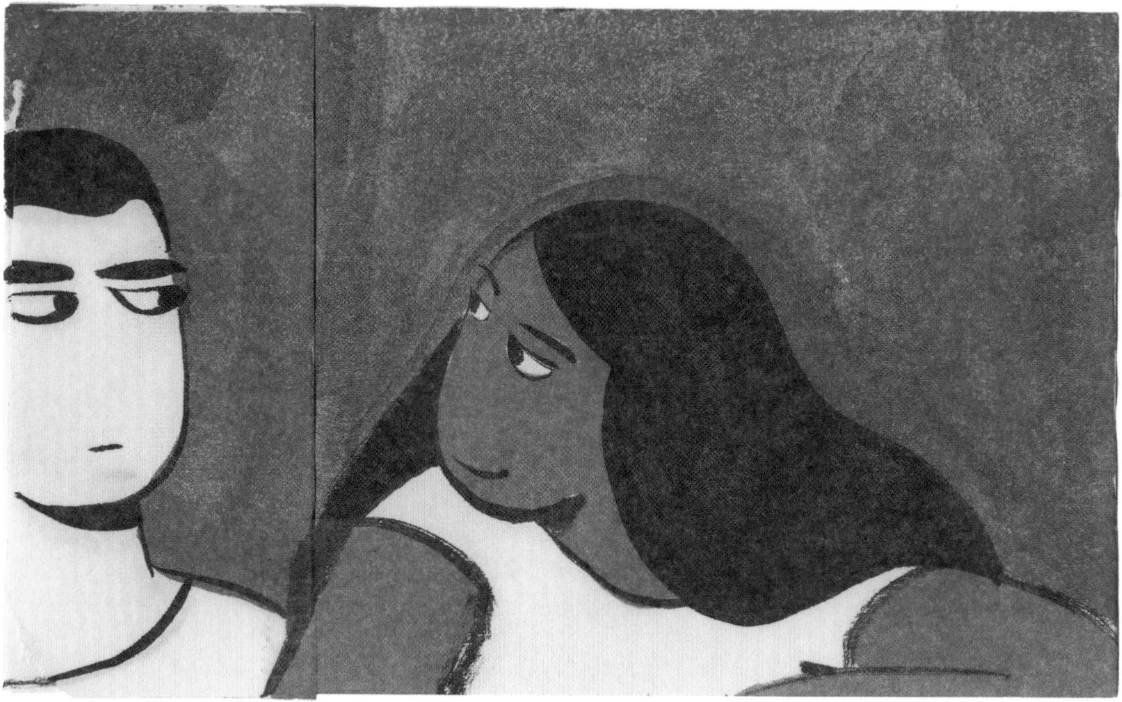

When you can't be anything other than you.

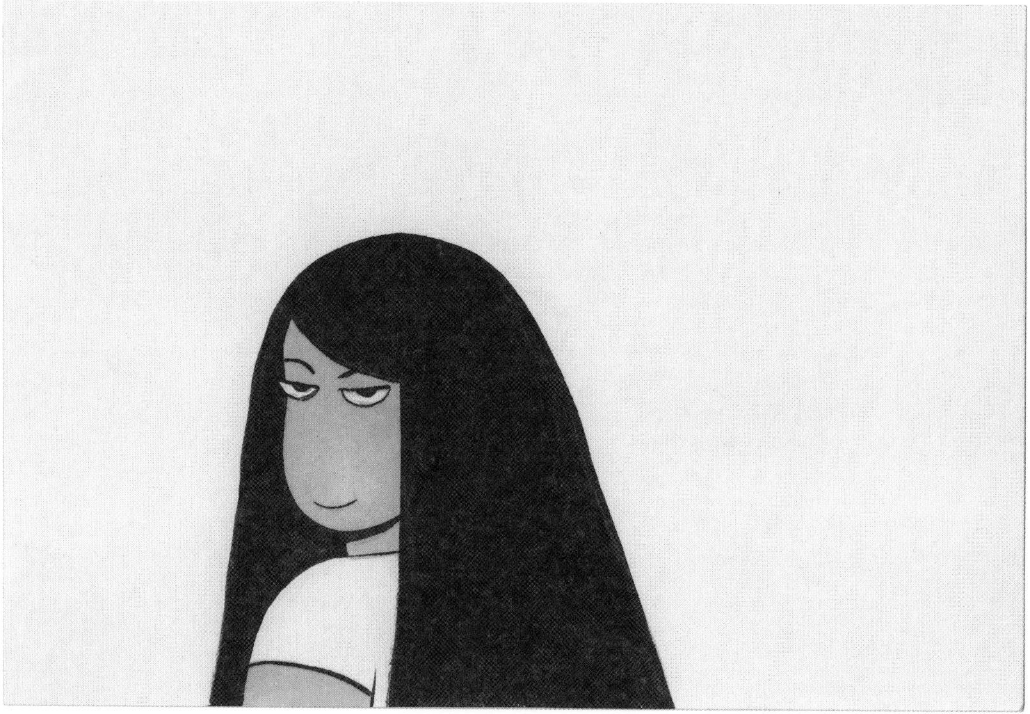

When you overhear your friend asking people
at the party if you've arrived yet
and you've been there for the last thirty minutes,
swirling your wine, mingling with boys, and eating
all the chips.

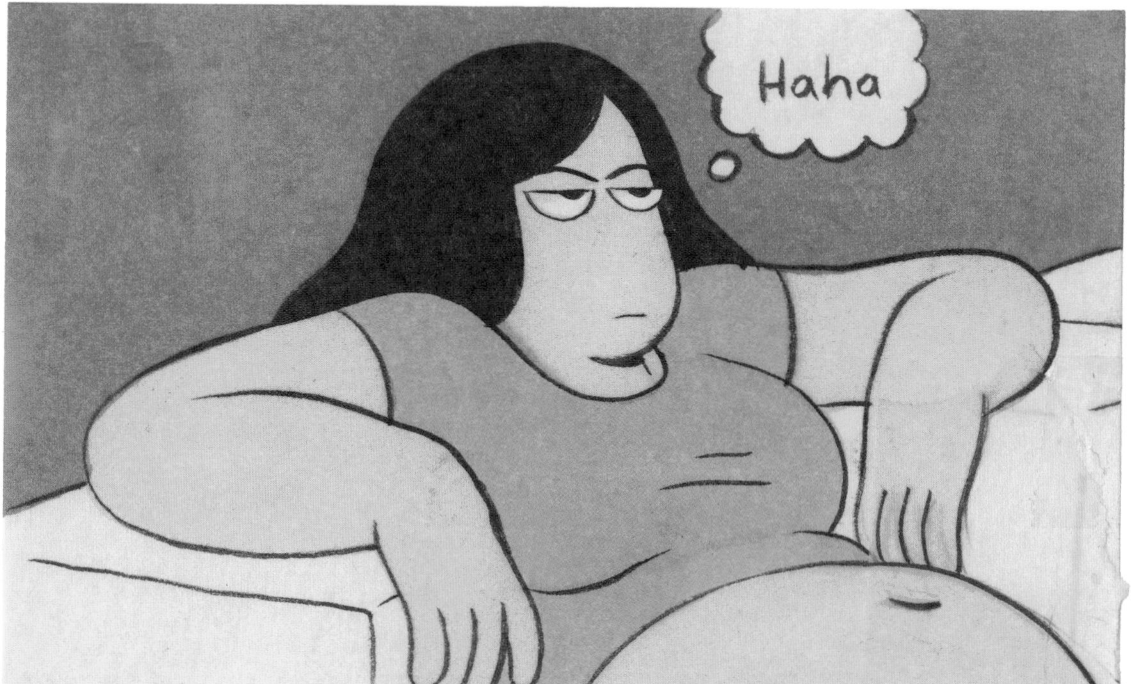
Haha

When you watch a funny TV show at home, alone.

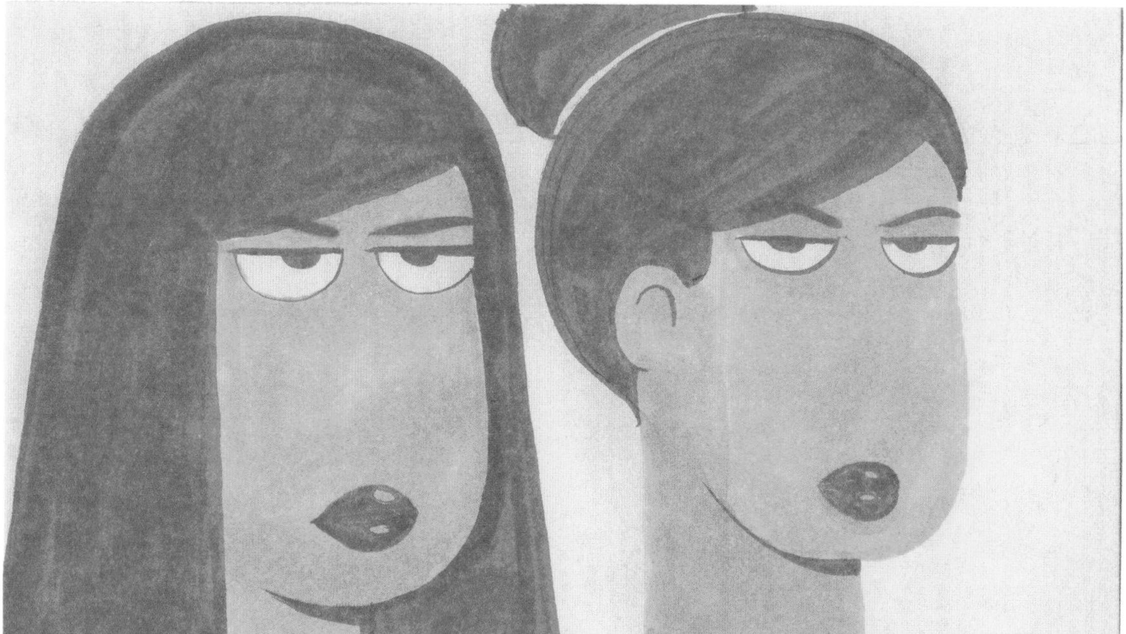

When you're trying a fun and flirty new look.

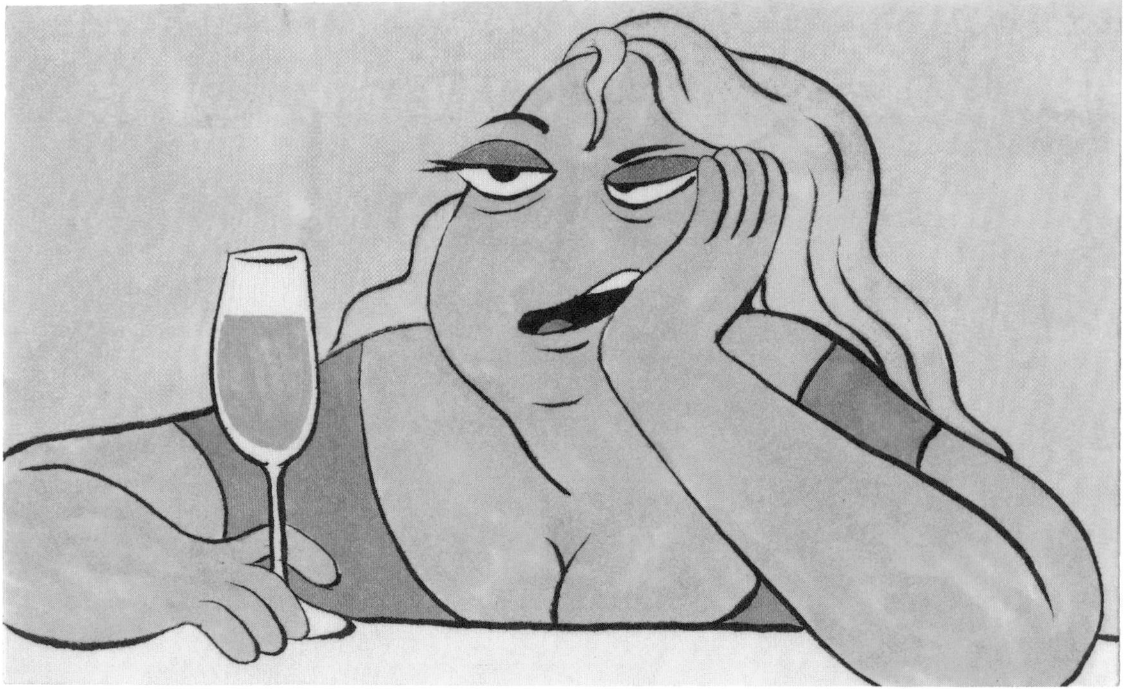

When you're at brunch with last night's eyeliner on your earlobe, telling him about how you really wanna start drinking less as you caress your eighth glass of mimosa and then immediately ask how big his dick is.

When he's complimenting your pussy skills but you're already well aware of your talents.

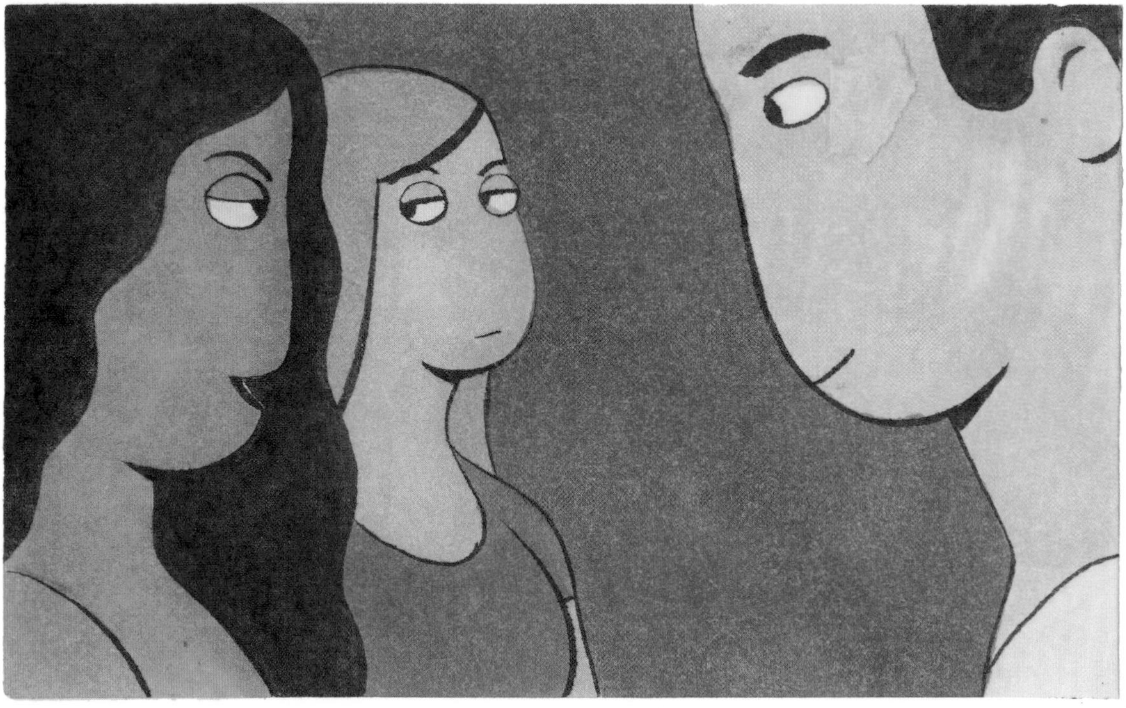

When you insisted on a ladies' night out because you're sick of men right now but this guy has been complimenting your mouth for the last twenty minutes so you're gonna take another shot and go down on him in the bathroom.

When you don't know yourself as well as
you thought.

When you're a troublemaker, according to others.

When you just exude cuntiness naturally.

CHAPTER 8

SMALL VICTORIES

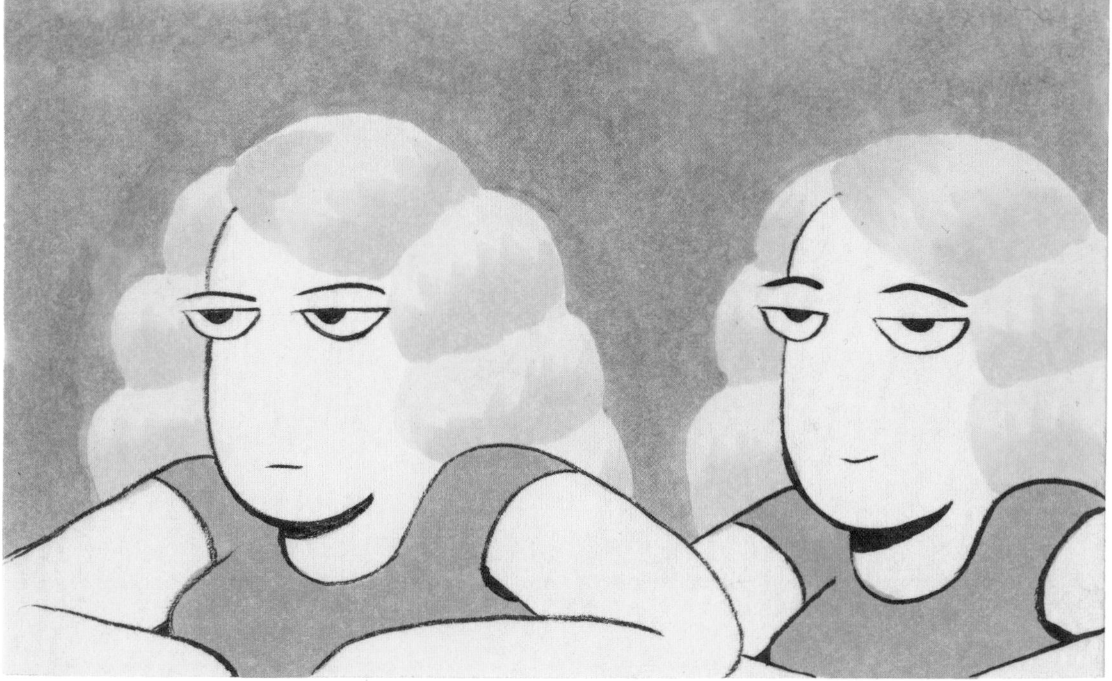

When you're in a bad mood and then you start thinking about all the men who've gotten boners
in public because you sexted them during work hours.

When someone else gets blamed for your fart.

When you're at a party and you run into that guy who ghosted you and now you have the whole evening to catch up with him and be BFFs with his new girlfriend.

When you crop dust a large group of unsuspecting people.

When your date snaps his fingers at the waitress, so you pick his pocket to tip her and go home with the hot bartender instead.

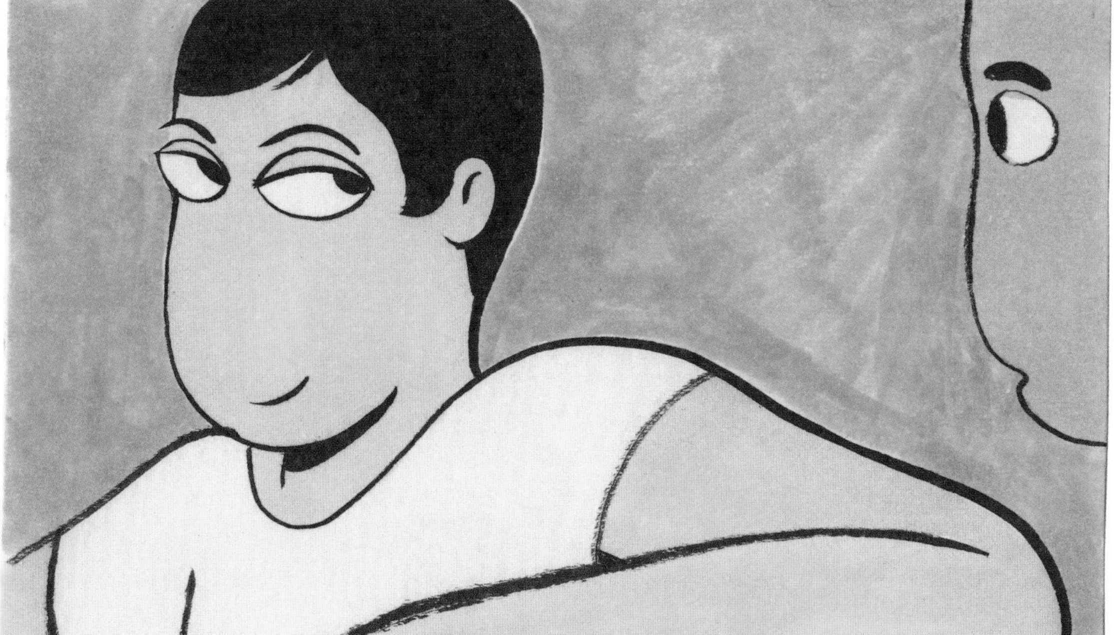

When another person looks dismayed by your existence and you revel in their discomfort.

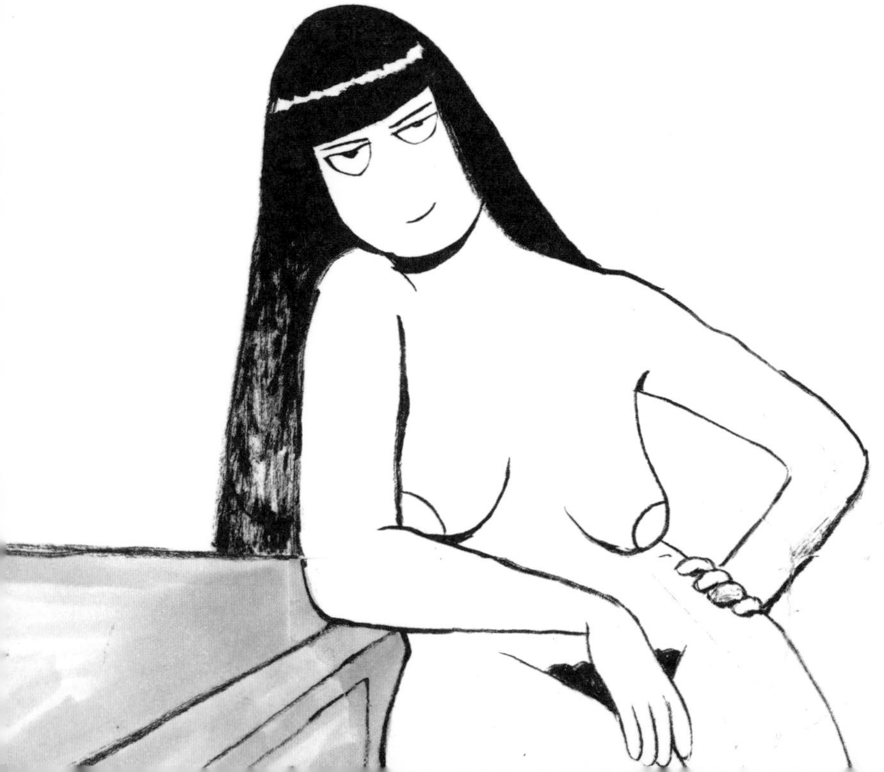

When you hide his keys so he has to bend over to look for them.

CHAPTER 9

(TRYING TO) FOLLOW THE RULES

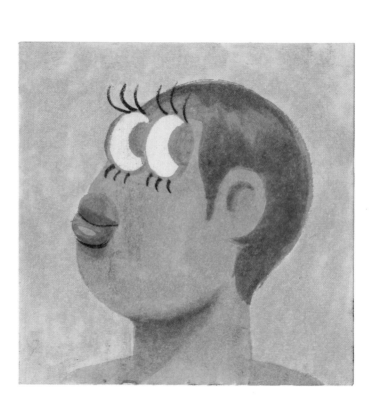

When you're trying to decide which one of your affairs to have over tonight.

When it's picture day at school but you prefer death over smiling.

When he loses the argument and you have to restore the peace.

When your manager tells you to smile more.

When your grandmother asks how work is going and you almost tell her about how great the sex party was last night and then remember she's referring to your accounting job.

CHAPTER 10
THE BODY

When you gotta make sure it's still firm.

When you try to understand the fascination.

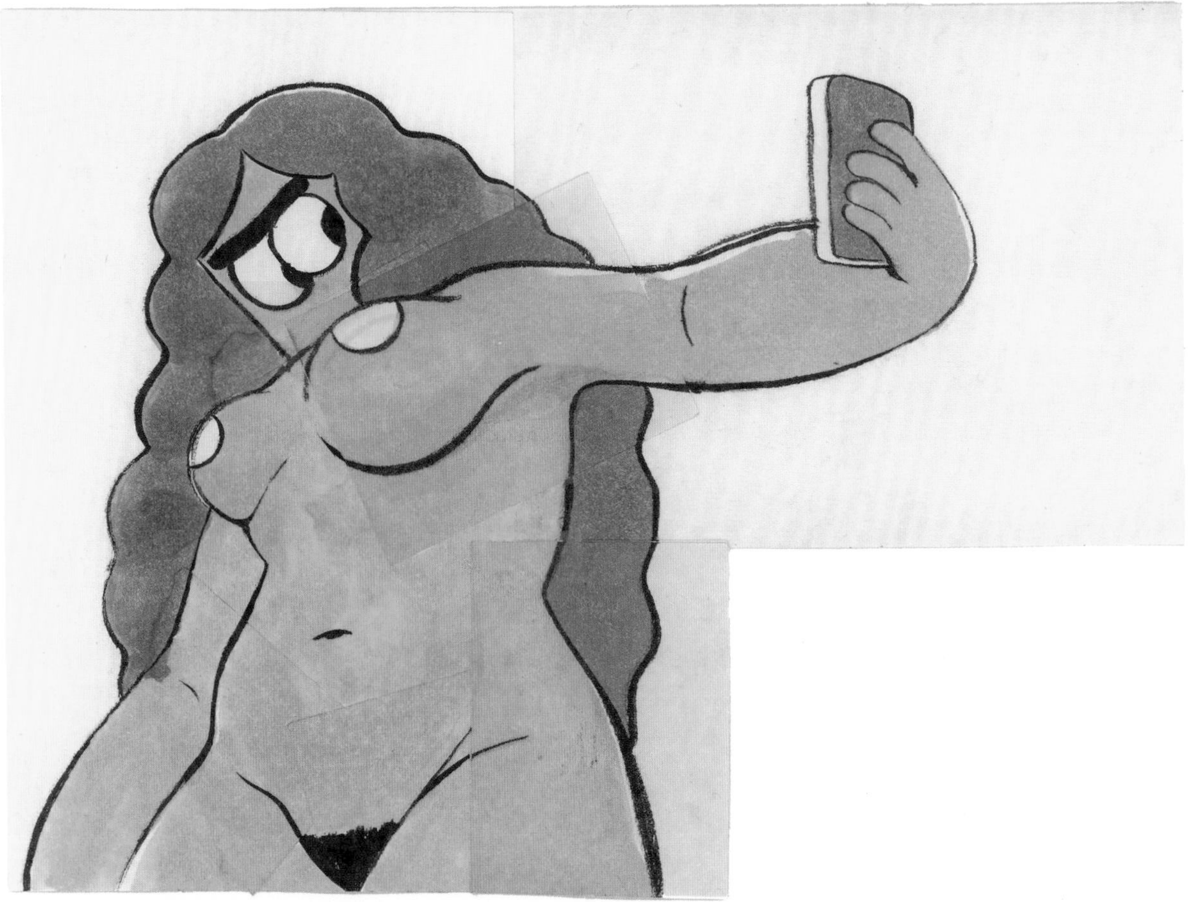

When the world must know how great
your tits are.

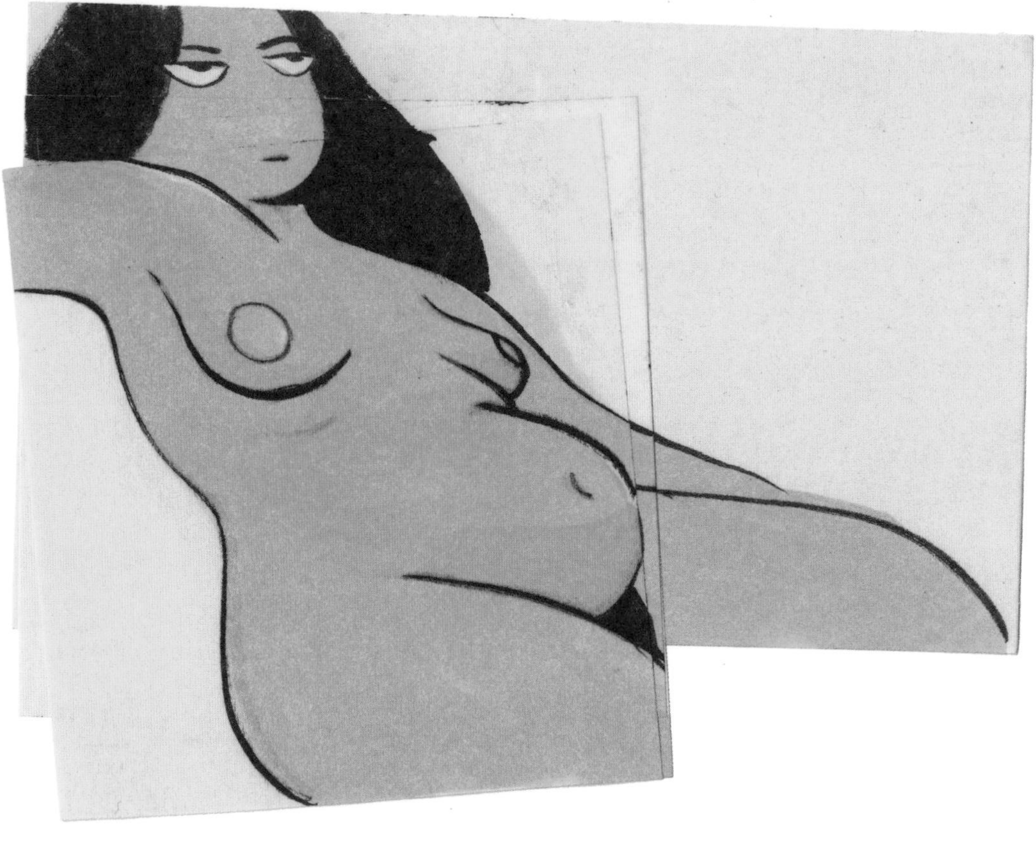

When you run out of fucks to give.

When you finally decide to go out but now you have to put on a bra.

When you're getting ready for work.

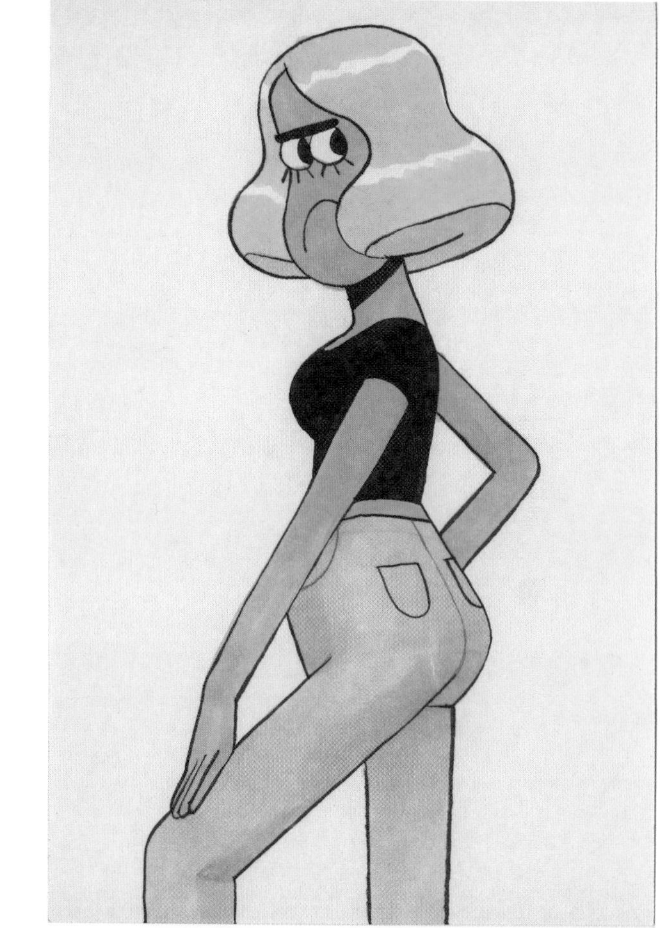

When you're in the fitting room.

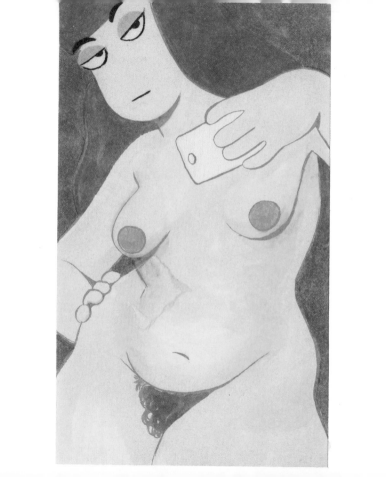

When you're waiting for the shower to warm up.

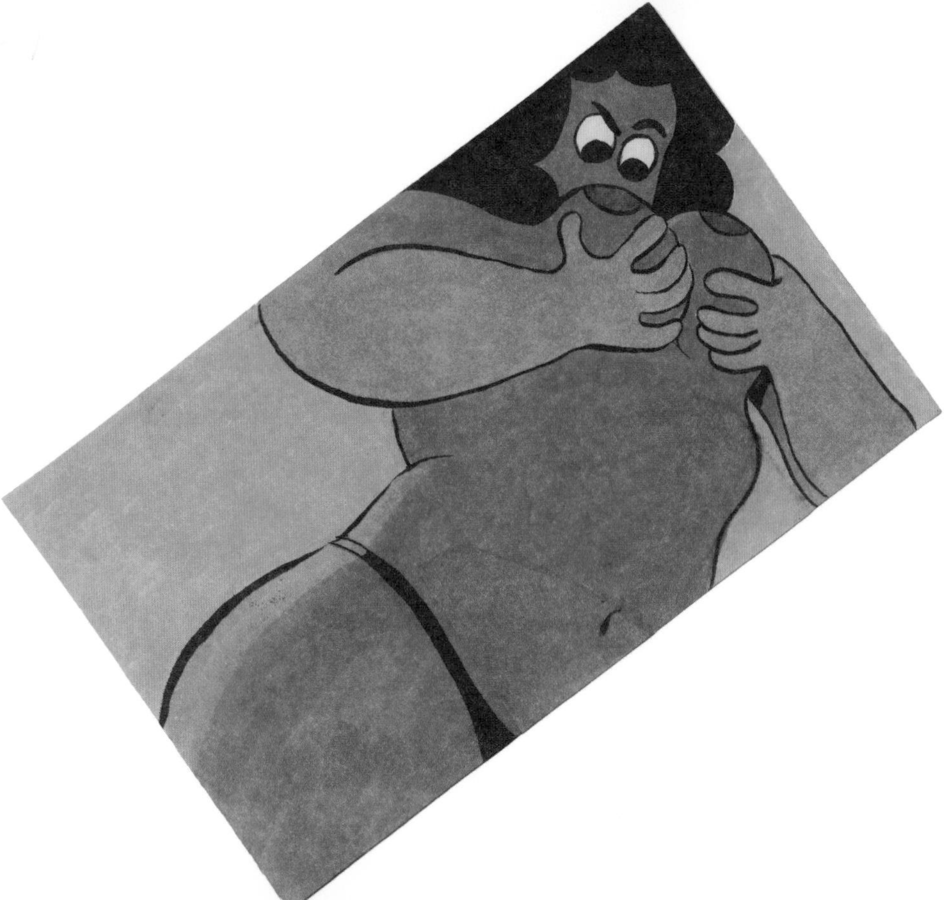

When you've had fully developed boobs for the last 18 years and you still look at 'em like they sprouted yesterday.

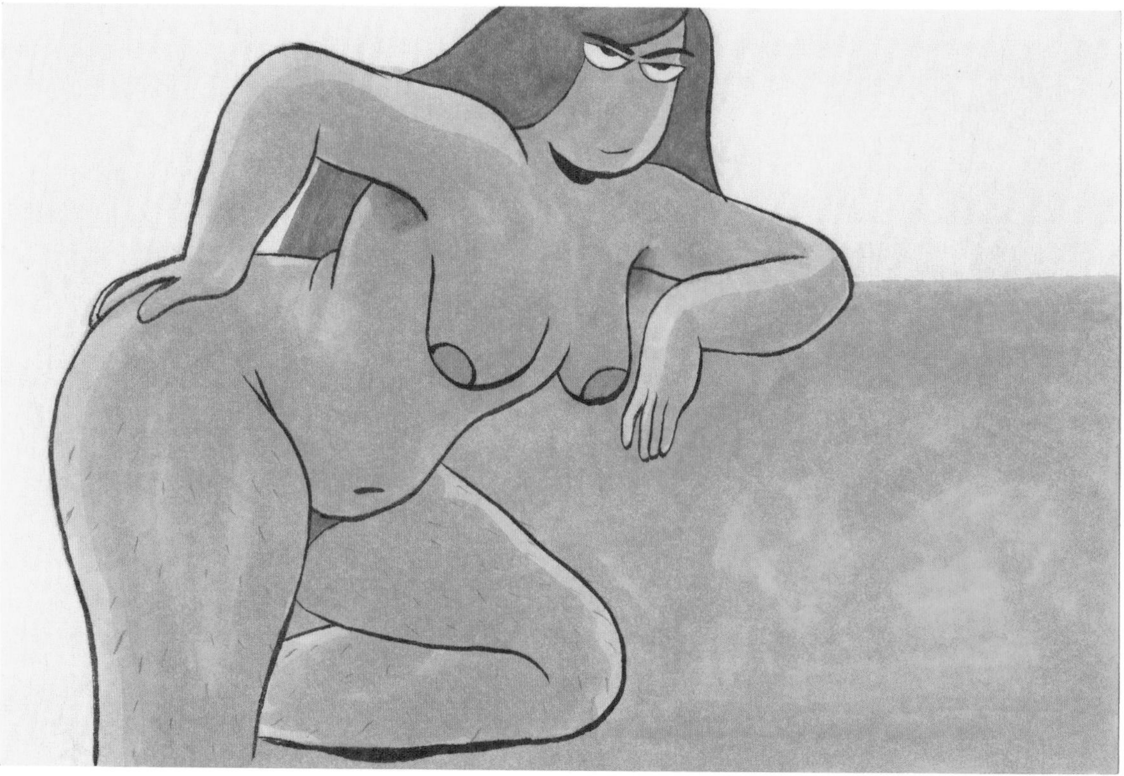

When you don't shave but you're smooth as fuck.

CHAPTER 11
SEX

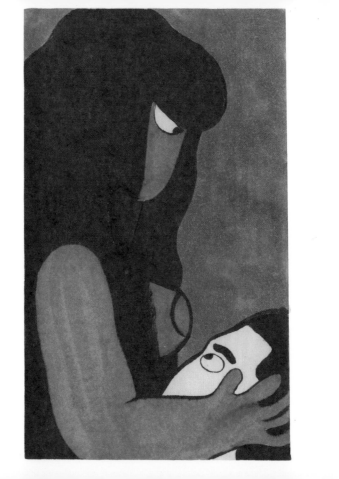

When you take advantage of the weak.

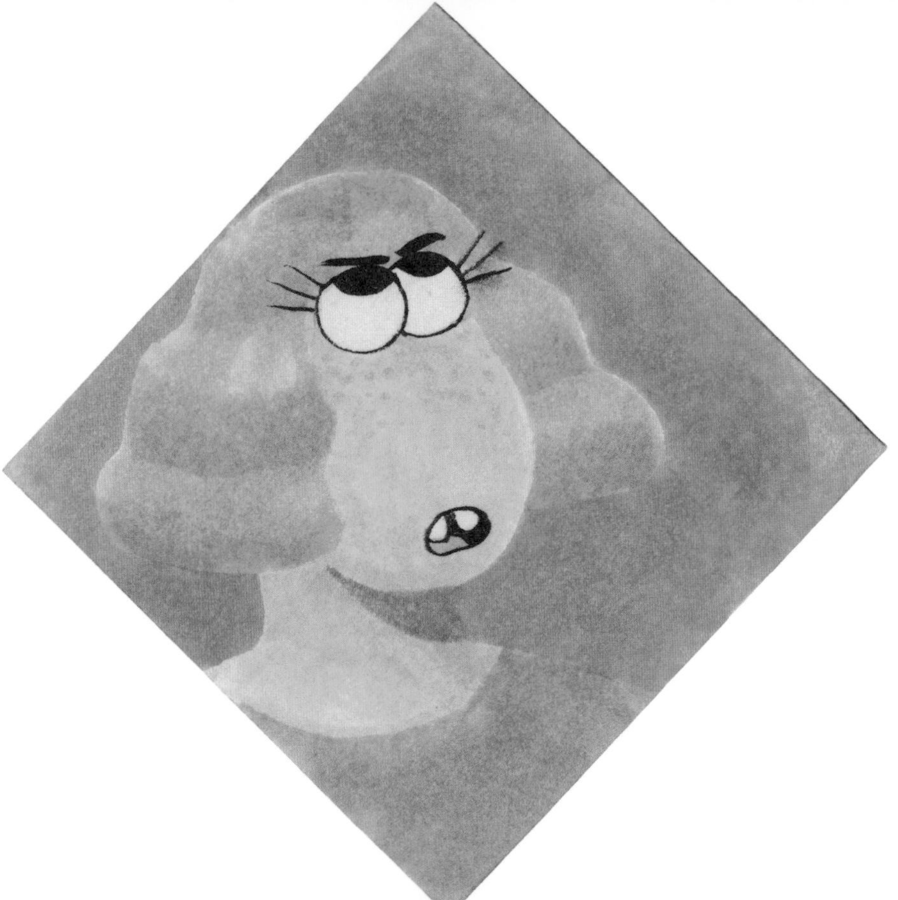

When you hear your neighbor upstairs orgasming
for the sixth time today.

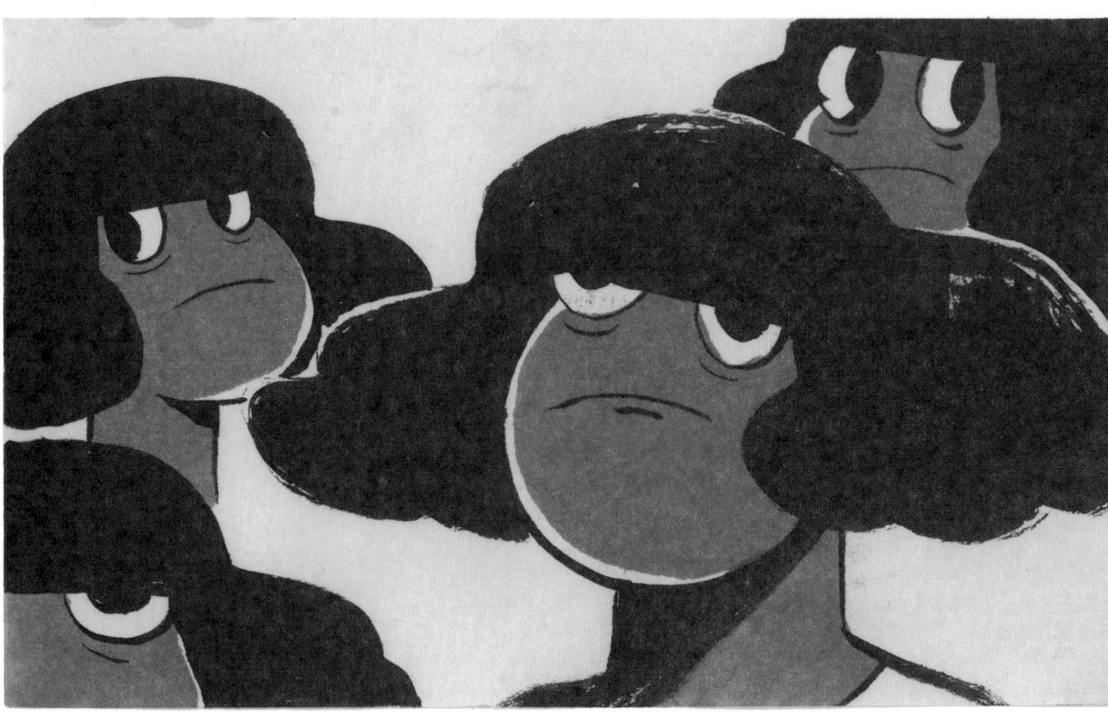

When you haven't had dick in a while.

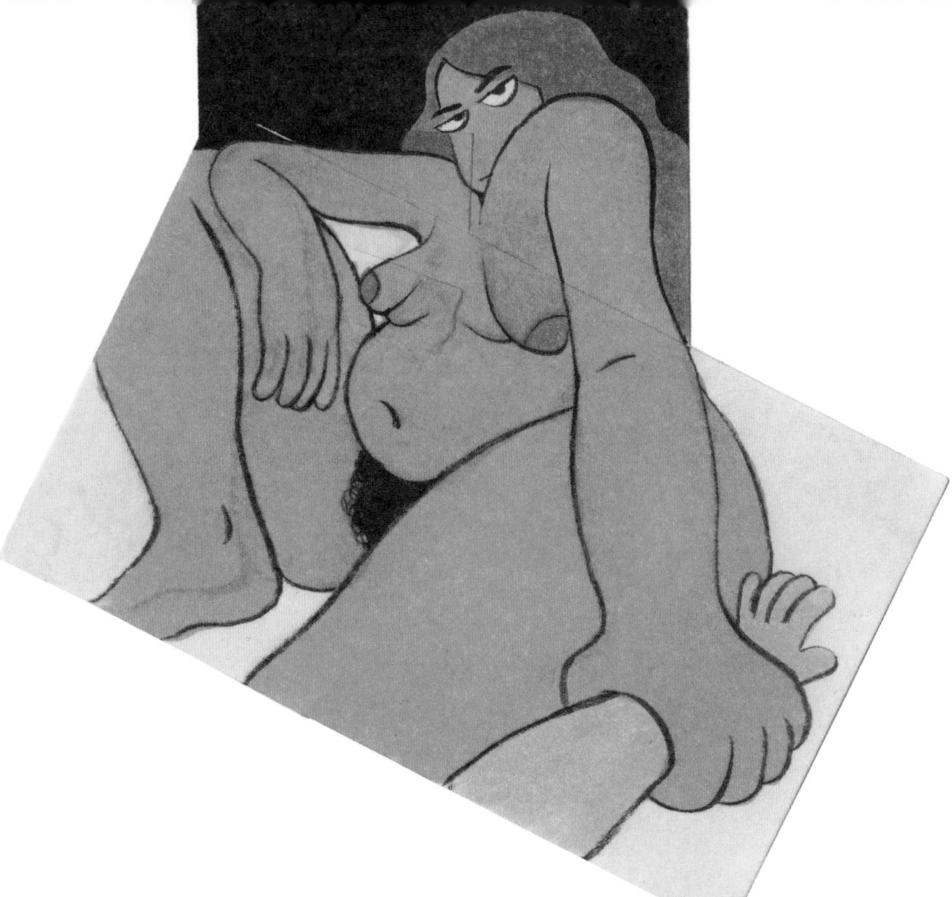

When he's being coy.

When all these men are just asking for it and you can't think with anything but your pussy.

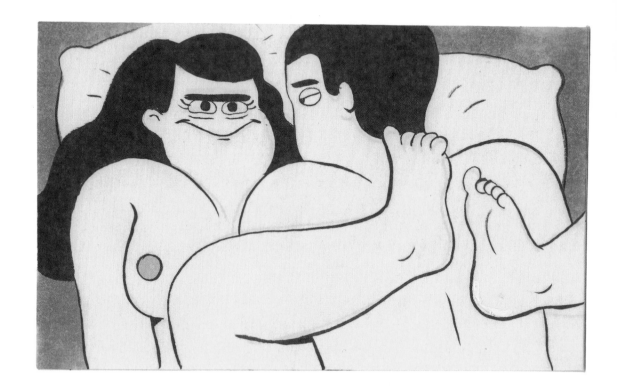

When you queef and he says it's not that funny, but it definitely is.

When he's hungry and you're thirsty.

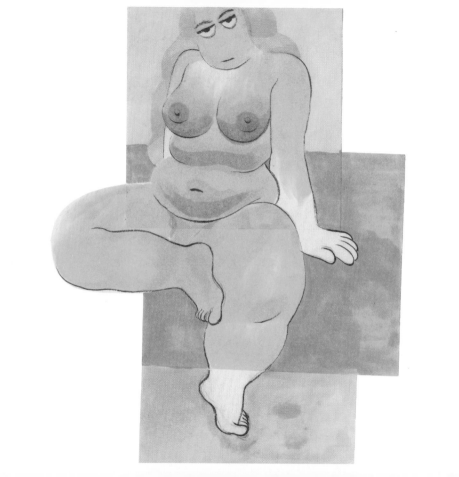

When you invite him over to watch something on Netflix but your WiFi is down.

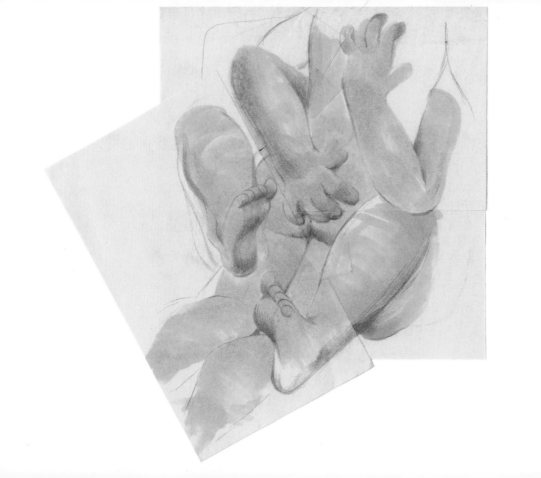

When the sex makes your toes curl.

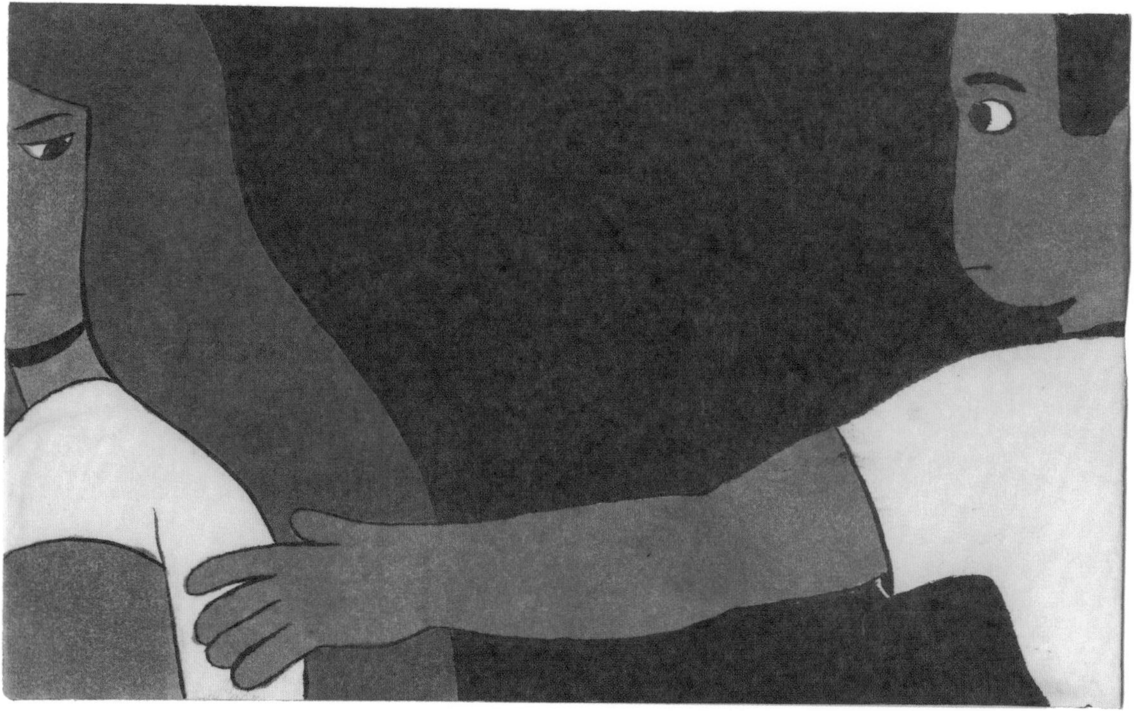

When he only reaches out when you pull away.

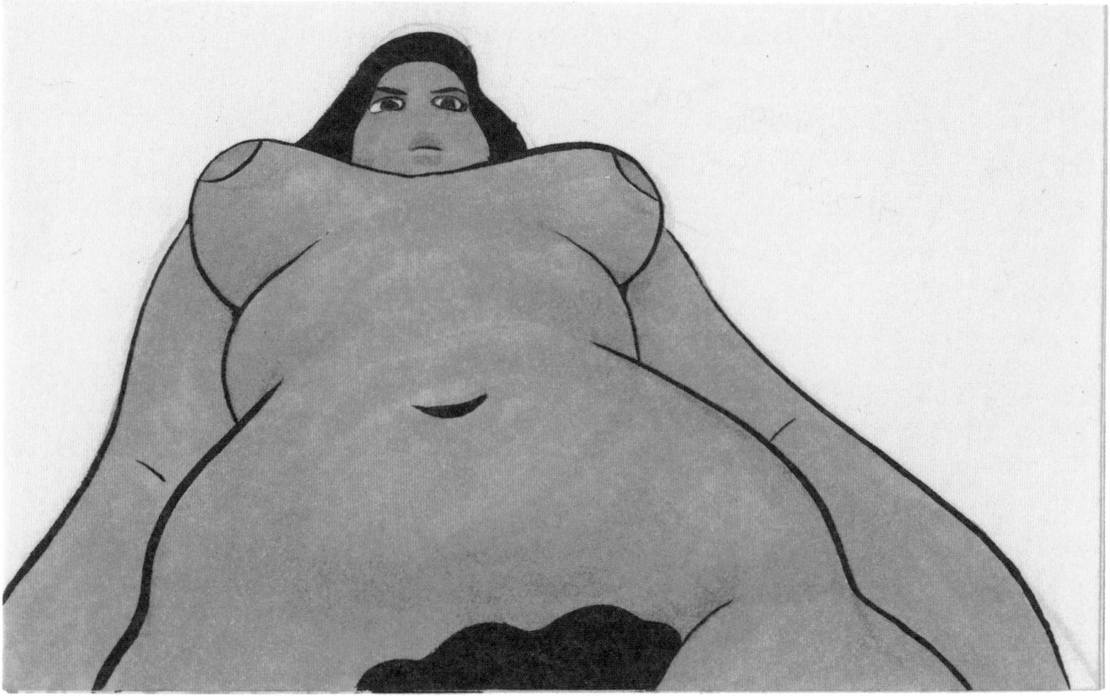

When it's not gonna eat itself.

When you wake up before he does.

When your friend asks what you did last night.

When your friend tells you what she did last night.

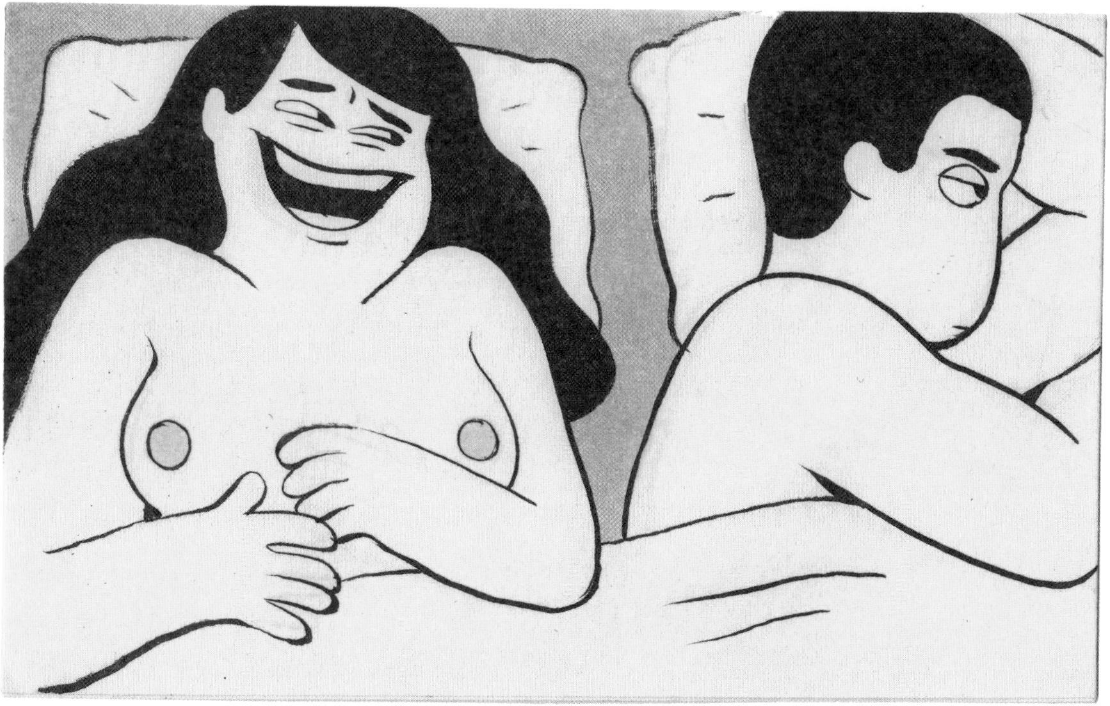

When he gives up because you can't
stop laughing about the queef.

.

When he's out of breath and wants to go again in twenty minutes but the Uber you called for him is only four minutes away.

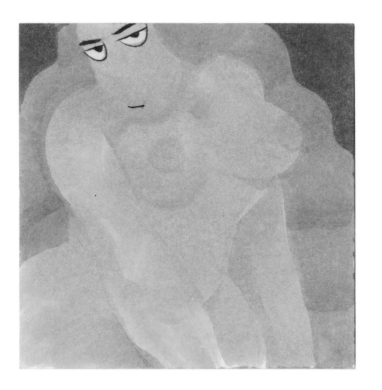

When you have all kinds of tricks
up your wizard sleeve.

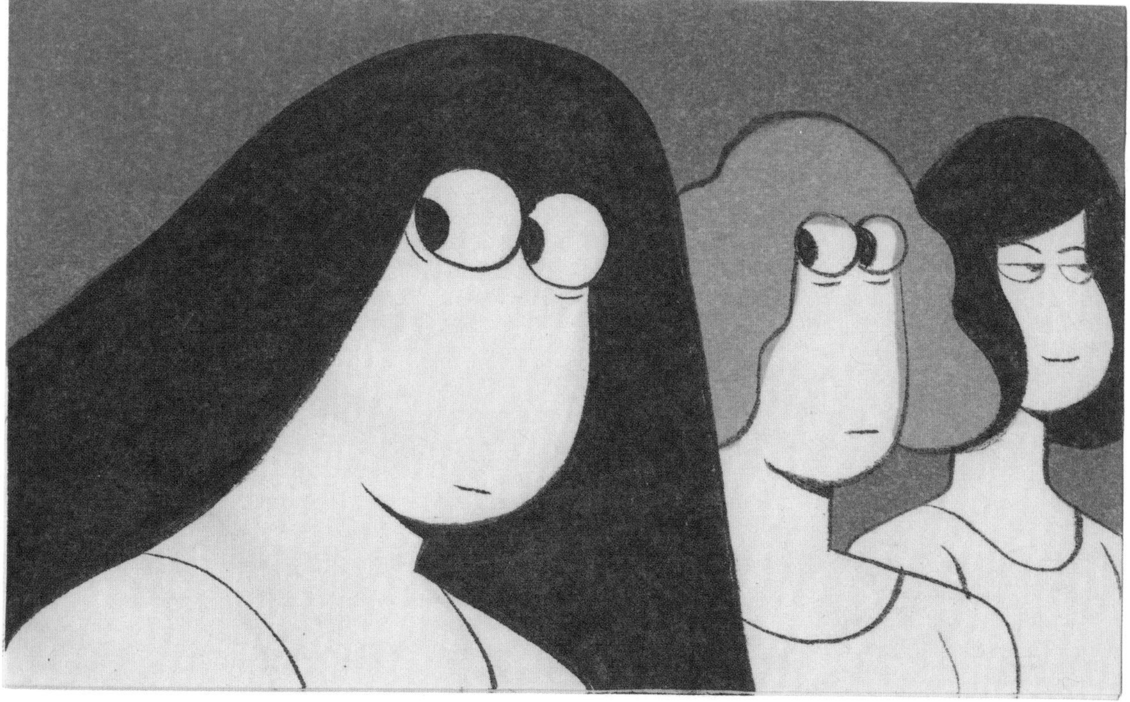

When your friend is giving an intense account of her recent near-death experience and you're just in the corner, thinking about cock.

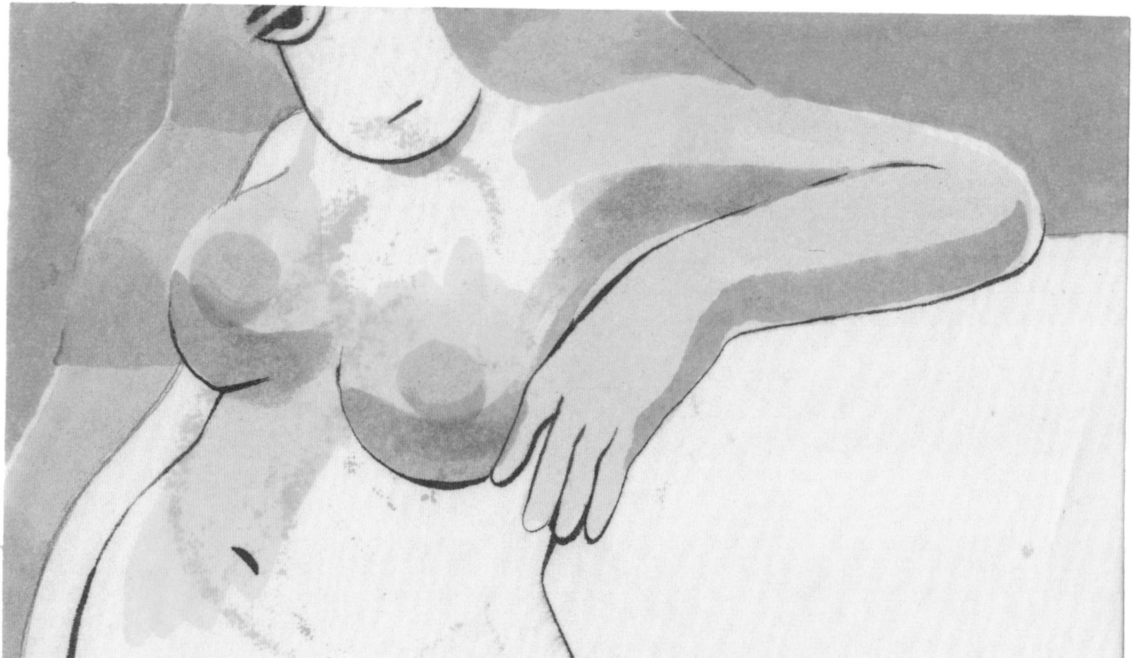

When he can't see you in more than one way.

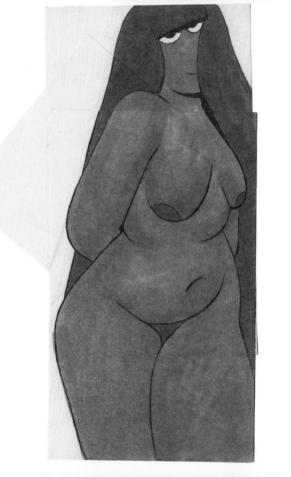

When your lover arrives.

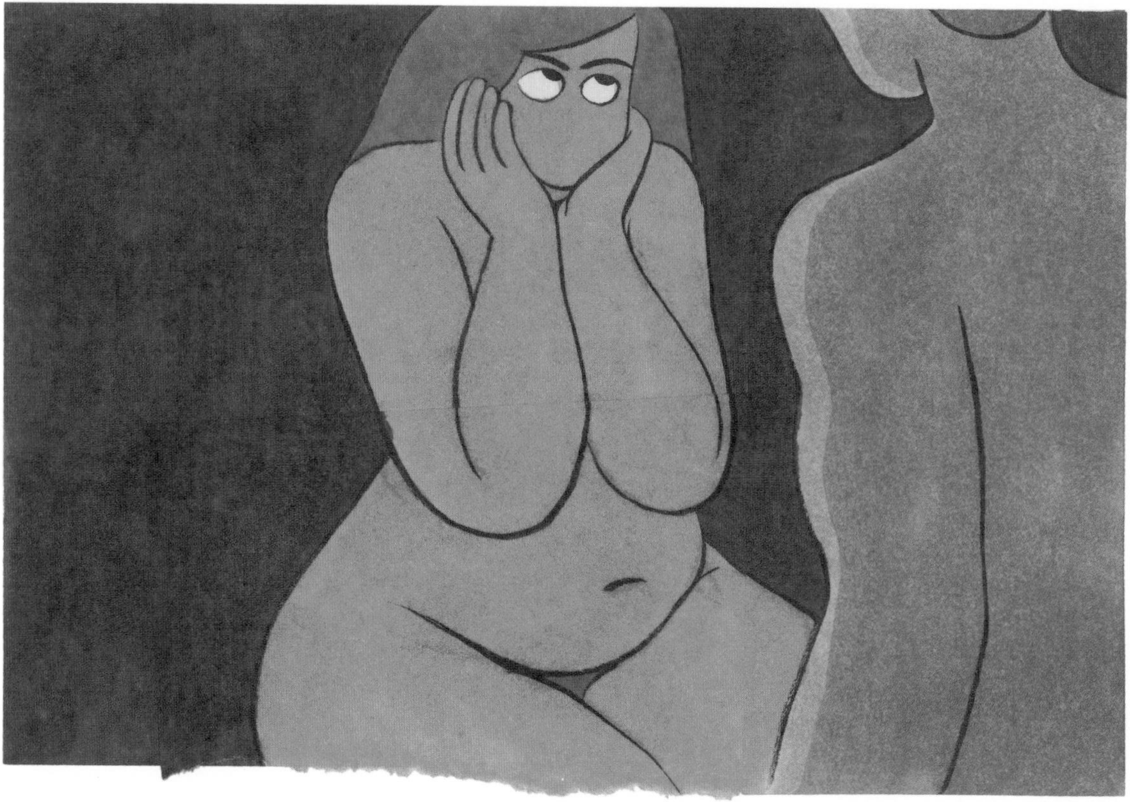

When you want to fuck
but don't want be seen.

When he says "goddamn" after you ride him into oblivion.

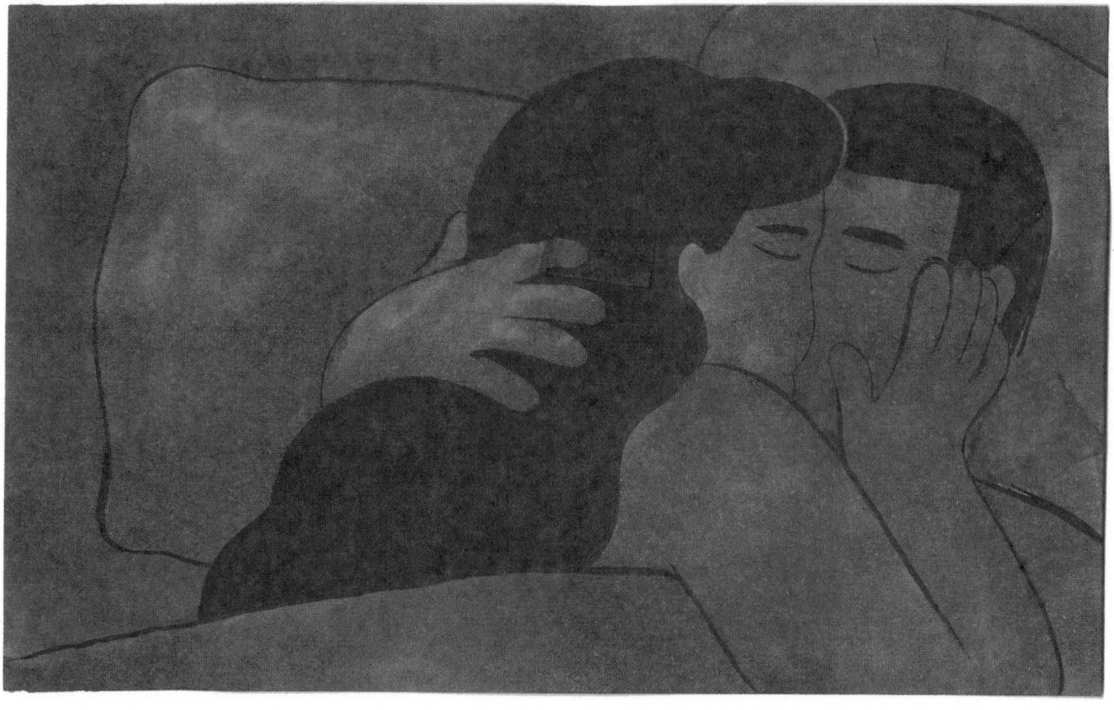

When you finally stop laughing about that queef.

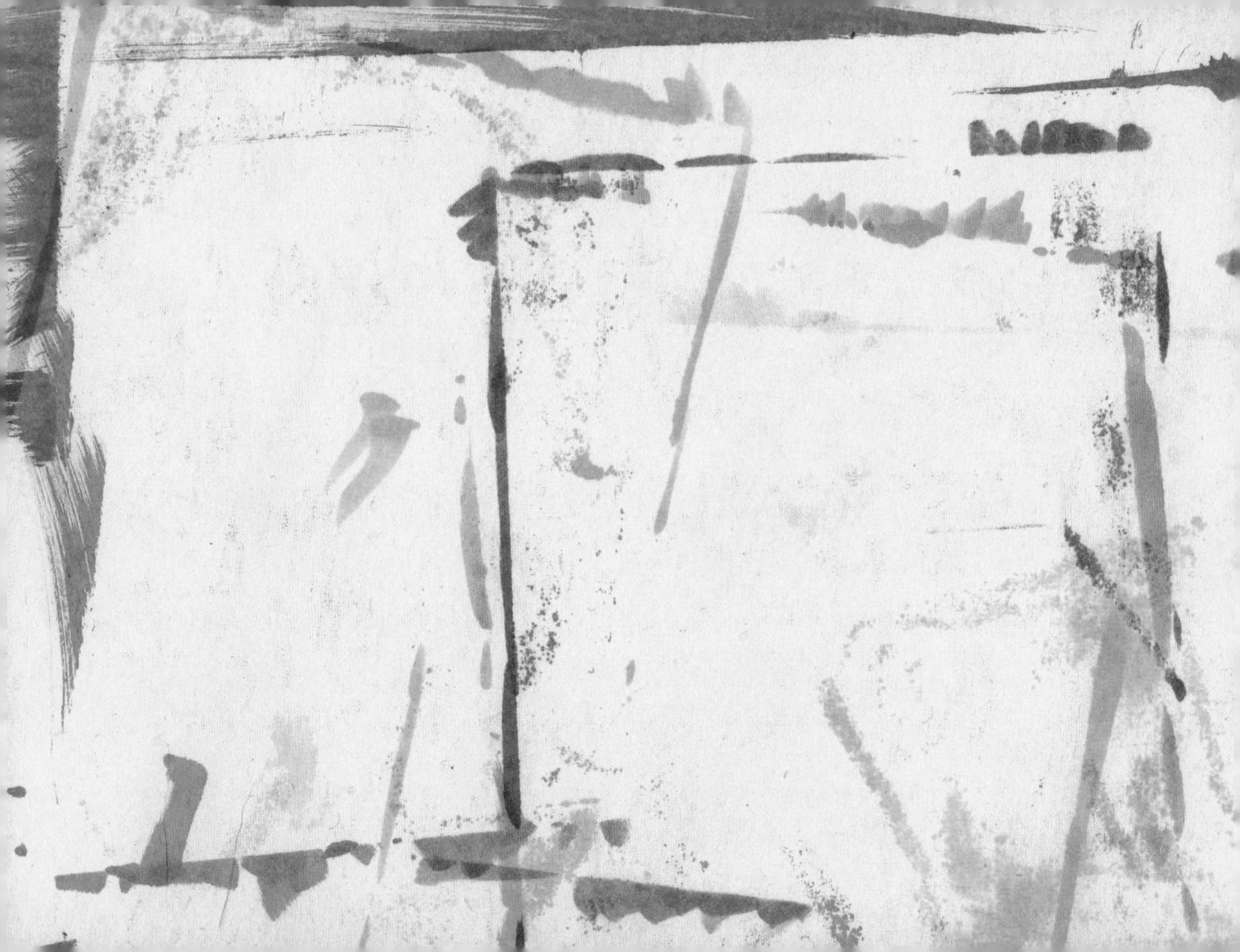

FANTAGRAPHICS BOOKS INC.
7563 Lake City Way NE
Seattle, Washington, 98115
www.fantagraphics.com

Editor / Associate Publisher: Eric Reynolds
Book Design & Production: Justin Allan-Spencer
Publisher: Gary Groth

ISBN 978-1-68396-469-8
Library of Congress Control Number 2021935664

First printing: November 2021
Printed in Hong Kong